MECHANICAL WITNESS

MECHANICAL WITNESS

A History of Motion Picture Evidence in U.S. Courts

LOUIS-GEORGES SCHWARTZ

OXFORD
UNIVERSITY PRESS

2009

OXFORD
UNIVERSITY PRESS

Oxford University Press, Inc., publishes works that further
Oxford University's objective of excellence
in research, scholarship, and education.

Oxford   New York
Auckland   Cape Town   Dar es Salaam   Hong Kong   Karachi
Kuala Lumpur   Madrid   Melbourne   Mexico City   Nairobi
New Delhi   Shanghai   Taipei   Toronto

With offices in
Argentina   Austria   Brazil   Chile   Czech Republic   France   Greece
Guatemala   Hungary   Italy   Japan   Poland   Portugal   Singapore
South Korea   Switzerland   Thailand   Turkey   Ukraine   Vietnam

Published by Oxford University Press, Inc.
198 Madison Avenue, New York, New York 10016

www.oup.com

Oxford is a registered trademark of Oxford University Press

Library of Congress Cataloging-in-Publication Data
Schwartz, Louis Georges.
Mechanical witness : a history of motion picture evidence in U.S.
courts / Louis-Georges Schwartz.
p. cm.
Includes bibliographical references and index.
ISBN 978-0-19-531505-9; 978-0-19-531506-6 (pbk.)
1. Video tapes in courtroom proceedings—United States. 2. Motion
pictures—Law and legislation—United States. 3. Evidence,
Demonstrative—United States. 4. Courts—United States. 5. Judicial
process—United States. I. Title.
KF8725.S39 2009
347.73'75—dc22   2008055740

1 3 5 7 9 8 6 4 2

Printed in the United States of America
on acid-free paper

Contents

MECHANICAL WITNESS

1

Introduction
After 100 Years of Evidentiary Film and Video

The introduction of evidentiary films into the U.S. courts in the 1910s marks a major shift in legal practice. In the century since, various kinds of film and video have been presented in court: recordings of crimes in progress, images that violate copyright law, tapes of expert witness testimony, reconstructions of events, and filmed confessions, to name a few examples. These uses of film and video have created a juridical motion picture practice substantially different from cinema, whether fictional or documentary, and semi-autonomous from the use of moving images in science and education. Despite the importance of evidentiary films in public life and their distinctive character, scholars have not often studied their use.

Ordinary language speaks of films and videos as more or less the same: as examples of the same media. Different institutions, however, use the media in dramatically different ways, creating very different texts. In common usage, "a film" and "a video" refer to a more or less closed text,[1] not, as in court, part of an argument that begins before the first image starts and ends after the last. Although a variety of institutions use moving images, cinema and television still provide a general model, and, in those contexts, films and videos are ordinarily presented as finished works, credited to a group of makers. Attorneys do not present films and videos as finished works, they offer evidentiary films into evidence during trials in attempts to prove their cases.

Showing evidentiary film or video at trial has become so common that we find it difficult to imagine a time when jurists regularly excluded motion pictures from evidence. From the early twentieth century through the 1910s, films were sometimes at issue in trials, for example in copyright cases. The films were not shown in court, instead, a witness who had seen a film testified about what he or she had seen (*Feeny*) (482). Courtrooms lacked the proper equipment and personnel to project films and judges distrusted film as a medium. As discussed in chapter 2, the first appellate decision concerning evidentiary film, *Feeny v. Young* (1920), deals with a woman who sued her obstetrician for having used images of her cesarean section in a documentary film without her consent. In the "interest of science" (*Feeny*) (482), Feeny had agreed to have her cesarean section filmed for the purpose of showing it to medical schools but had not agreed to its exhibition for the general public. The film, *Birth*, had played at "two of the leading moving picture houses in New York" (*Feeny*) (482). To prove her case Feeny had to demonstrate to the jury that *Birth* in fact contained images of her operation. The trial judge would not allow the film to be shown in court for purposes of identifying Feeny. Projecting a film in court was almost unthinkable at this time, as is made clear in the appellate court's statement that although the film itself had been in the courtroom, "the picture naturally could not there be thrown on the screen" (*Feeny*) (482). The court held that the proper means for entering the contents of the film into evidence would have been through the testimony of a witness who had seen the film.

The courts slowly established a precedent whereby films were defined as a series of photographs and admissible under the same principle allowing the use of still pictures (*Gulf Life v. Stossel*) (128). The third chapter traces the judiciary's regulation of their use and interpretation in the 1940s and 1950s. In this period, the types of evidentiary film proliferated as lawyers invented new uses. Films could be offered as evidence both of directly visible matters and of facts that could only be inferred from what could be seen. Moreover, evidentiary films varied in their value as proof according to how they were used. The courts could not develop a single set of rules governing their use because, although they treated motion pictures as a single technology, evidentiary films were used in a variety of legal maneuvers; sometimes films fit into established evidentiary categories, other times films generated new categories of evidence, subject to new regulations (*Kennedy*) (426).

Courts offered two new definitions for film as a medium: jurists construed films either as physical proof (*Gulf Life v. Stossel*) (128) or as pictorial communication of witness testimony (*International Union v. Paul S. Russell*) (470). Both kinds had to be authenticated by a testimonial foundation and the credibility of a given film varied according to how that foundation was laid. When an image was presented as proof, witnesses had to attest to its veracity with testimony about its making and projection. When a film was shown as pictorial communication of witness testimony, the medium was not supposed to make it better proof than what could have been said on the stand. Two theories of truth, one based on seeing evidence and the other on hearing testimony, came into conflict. Within this crisis, evidentiary films held the problematic position of an objective form of sight that, unlike cinematic seeing, never implies a seeing subject as its terminus.

Lawyers soon learned to invoke scenarios that could have happened before the camera was turned on or beyond the image's frame as a means of falsifying the image (*DeBattiste v. Anthony Laudadio & Son et al.*) (42). The fact-value of this juridical mode of vision was threatened by its very potential for reproduction since the repetition of a filmed image leaves behind the context in which it was taken. By making claims about that context, attorneys could invalidate arguments given when a film was entered into evidence. The courts responded by imposing various strictures on evidentiary films to ensure both their objectivity and their repeatability, but the problem of repetition and context would return once television networks started regularly broadcasting evidentiary videos.

In late 1960s and early 1970s the introduction in the United States of the first commercial, portable video recording system, the Sony Portapak®, increased the legal community's interest in the use of motion picture evidence. Video was more readily integrated into trials than film for several reasons. Showing a videotape is less disruptive of trial procedure than projecting a film (for example, the courtroom lights need not be dimmed). Video is easier to authenticate than film; there is no need for testimony about the reliability of the laboratory that developed it, because videos come out of the camera ready to screen. By the mid-1970s, the mass manufacture of ever more portable, progressively simpler, and less expensive videotape equipment rendered the use of moving images in court even more attractive. These advantages incited courts to replace film with video and use it much more extensively than they had ever used celluloid. The period generated a number of policy statements, guidelines, and manuals on the use of videotaped evidence at trial, justifying the use of video through social science.

During the 1970s, courts considered video a purveyor of fact (*United States of America v. Guerrero*) (867). In addition to framing video so as to be admissible on the same basis as film, jurists saw video as a very desirable convenience for presenting depositions and recording trials. The legal community believed that the use of video depositions would speed up lengthy jury trials (McCrystal). They were therefore motivated to incorporate the medium into the infrastructure of the courts. Guidelines indicating forms (editing, camera angles, and so on) to be followed in official tapes were established by government organizations such as the Federal Justice Center (*Guidelines*). Video production manuals for lawyers show the sophisticated strategies for the use of video that were developed in the wake of the acceptance of the medium in courts. This mode of representation was, in effect, a pragmatically determined semiotic for legal moving images.

Appellate court decisions show that video appeared as a window onto events rather than as a particular evidentiary medium (*United States of America v. Guerrero*) (867). Abscam, a 1978 investigation into political corruption generating hours of video evidence to expose political corruption in local and federal governments, represents the high point of the courts' confidence in videos. Some of the tapes presented by the prosecution in Abscam were broadcast on television news. Journalists treated the story as a scandal and accepted the prosecution's interpretation of the tapes, as if video were a universal medium of truth. By 1992, the courts' interpretation of particular videotapes and of the medium in general would have to negotiate the television audience's interpretations.

Over the course of six decades, the courts came to consider film and video as the most reliable form of evidence. In the early 1990s, the Rodney King case precipitated a shift in the value of motion picture evidence. When a videotape of a motorist's beating by police following a pursuit on the freeway was broadcast on television, it seemed to prove wrongdoing on the part of the LA police officers involved. However, although the video of the incident was shown in court, the officers were found not guilty.

Despite the importance of these developments for both legal studies and a general history of motion pictures, scholars have not done much work on evidentiary films and videos. Film scholars have not studied the juridical use of film and video because "film studies" has a strong tendency to understand itself as "cinema studies" or "cinema and media studies," taking artistic and entertainment practices as a universal model for all uses of the moving image.

The cinema refers to a particular set of institutions, not to the moving images in general.[2] When film scholars do attend to the use of films and videos as evidence, they assume that images shown in court work in the same way as the cinema. Film studies mistakes a particular institution, cinema, for the universal moving image. The conventions of cinema differ from those followed in court as do the rules about what conclusions are permissible. The same is true of television and video art. Legal scholars have not addressed the particularities of moving images in court extensively because, from their point of view, films and videos are part of the general category of "evidence." In the 1970s and 1980s, jurists produced many manuals and guides for producing evidentiary video, but they did not treat the history of motion picture evidence.

In 1992, the Los Angeles uprising following the first trial of the police officers who beat Rodney King should have provided an occasion for film scholars to think about the courts' use of evidentiary video. Some did attempt to respond, drafting a resolution condemning the verdict at the Society for Cinema Studies annual conference in Pittsburg. The SCS resolution called the tape "powerful visual evidence" (SCS) (2) and attributed the uprising in Los Angeles to "the jury's deliberate refusal to 'see' this visual evidence the way that most of us—regardless of color— saw these images" (SCS) (2). The statement clearly assumes that images function in the same way on television and in court. Both the noun-phrase "visual evidence" and the verb "to see" are used as if they meant the same thing on television and at trial. The word "seeing" is offered to the reader unconditioned by any institutional frame. The quotation marks around "see" in the resolution imply that the seeing required of the jury was something other than a simple act of visual cognition, but the sentence states that the jury did not look at the visual evidence correctly: if they had seen properly, in the way that comes naturally to everyone everywhere, they could not have acquitted the officers. The writers of the statement imply a collective subject that structures its sight with common sense. Yet in court, evidentiary videos do not terminate in any such seeing subject much less the subject of common sense. Here, the question of whether a subject comes attached to a sight or a sight is given as prior to any subject is forgotten because the question of institutional criteria for truth has been forgotten.

The resolution goes on to say that the jury saw the tape "in slow motion, analytically—as the defense supplied a 'reading' of the appropriateness of each officer's reaction. This demonstrates how close readings can incur misreadings" (SCS) (2). Here again, the resolution's terms are unframed, not linked to a context. One cannot tell whether the resolution implies that all close readings are of the same kind, that they "can" err in similar ways, or what criteria a reading would have to meet in order to not be a misreading. Here again, the authors seem to miss the possibility that what counts as a correct reading or interpretation might vary in different institutional contexts. The SCS statement comes to the same conclusions about evidentiary videos in court as the prosecution in the first trial of the police officers that beat King. They claim that the tape should only ever be understandable in one way: the way it was understood by its first television audiences, as an image of injustice.

While I share the resolution's "outrage" that "Blacks' experience of police brutality does not count" (SCS) (2), the generality of the resolution's language and its undifferentiated attack on close reading concern me. Not all close readings follow the same protocols, and thus they can only be called misreadings with respect to particular criteria that have their own history. I feel that it is important to investigate the possibility that such "misreadings" are facilitated by something in the juridical mode of interpretation beyond the jury's putative bias.

My project started as an inquiry into the juridical protocols of interpretation that allowed the jury to participate in such a "misreading." The verdict, and the intensity of the reaction to its injustice, gave me a fleeting glimpse of two different images, both recorded on the same segment of videotape. The image that appeared on television was a direct, incontrovertible recording of indefensible violence by the State's repressive apparatus. The image framed by the video monitor in the courtroom appeared to be ambiguous; the jury could reasonably doubt that it proved the officer's guilt in the matter at trial.

Film and video are not technologies transparently adopted by the courts to meet the need for certain kinds of evidence. Motion pictures brought their own problems of proof into court and shifted long-established assumptions about evidence. The language of the first appellate court decisions on the propriety of presenting evidentiary films evinces the strangeness of the moving image for jurists in the first decades of the twentieth century. At first the courts were unsure about how an evidentiary film should be made or presented to a jury. Once the courts had established that the precedent permitting photographs to be used as evidence also made films admissible, attorneys began to develop strategies for presenting and contesting moving images so as to make them appear as either physical proof of an event or as pictorial testimony to it. As courts grew more and more familiar with the use of evidentiary films, they began to treat properly authenticated motion pictures as the best proof. When videotape was introduced into the courtrooms in the 1970s, the moving image was no longer questioned as a means for bringing the truth into court. By the early 1990s attorneys had found lines of attack, such as those used by the defense attorneys in the Rodney King case (*California v. Powell et al.*), to shake juridical confidence in the image.

Film studies has traditionally been very attentive to the specificity of the film medium.[3] Unlike the courts, film scholars maintained a strict distinction between film and video. The field also works on institutional differences between different film industries and genres. However, very little attention has been paid to the use of motion pictures in non-cinematic institutions, despite the fact that film scholars have been loudly declaring the death of cinema for some time now.[4] The cinema remains the basic model for film study's understanding of the moving image. Most film scholars see noncinematic or paracinematic uses of film or video as variations, if not deviations, from cinematic practice.

Film scholars have tended to posit the formal aspects of film that set it apart from other representational media as the essence of moving pictures. Even when they claim to be making genealogies, they mistake the contingent condition of cinema for the structure of the moving image. Seen as a medium with an essence, film's uses are understood as expressing that essence in various ways, but all the uses are understood as closely related. For most film scholars, the use of evidentiary film and video in court must be based on the indexical potential of the medium as elaborated by certain film theorists.

As in many interpretations of *cinematic* moving images, evidentiary film and video come to connote indexicality, but, in *court*, the cinema of indexicality is not the same as in film theory. In the cinema such indexicality is an implicit result of the medium itself and works to give the spectator an impression of reality.[5] In court, film's indexicality is a result of the combination of a particular image and the testimony authenticating it, making the process of creating a particular image explicit. Evidentiary film's indexicality functions to purvey the facts of an event to the jury.

For television audiences, the King tape's indexicality was implicitly established and the tape's vision implied a subject with a common sensibility. In court, the tape did not function as an index that the police involved had broken with authorized procedure. The tape functioned as proof that the beating occurred only insofar as it appeared as a seeing detached from any seeing subject, allowing those present in court to see the beating for themselves. Yet the very marks of historical trauma on the tape, the limitations that give the image its power on television, imply a subject embedded in the situation in which the tape was shot. Entering the tape into evidence rendered those marks irrelevant. The materiality of vision disappears in the process of translating the image into a set of facts. The defense controlled the translation of the tape into facts through the use of testimony. Because the prosecution offered the tape to prove something that was not entirely visible (i.e., the use of excessive force), the defense was able to solicit testimony that the image suggested something else.

Formally, the cinema encourages the use of motion pictures to produce subjectivity and affect, but the courts proscribe such effects. Evidentiary films and videos must function as nonsubjective seeing and any affect they contain must be screened out as prejudicial. In U.S. courts, the jury works to try the facts of a case and Anglo-American jurisprudence draws a bright line between affect and fact.

The specificity of juridical use of films and videos is an important consideration for "film theory" because it shows that motion pictures framed by different institutions do not entail the same concepts. Although film theory generally takes the cinema as its object, it tends to reach conclusions about the use of images in society at large. In doing so, it formulates propositions about the motion picture outside of any institutional context. The moving image, however, always appears within a particular institution and is conditioned by that institution's pragmatic requirements and history. Any general theory of our society of images must describe the use of images in particular institutions.

The study of the use of evidentiary moving images in courts should shift the center of film studies. Motion pictures appear differently in different frames; in addition, what counts as a motion picture and how this category is divided changes from institution to institution. This contingency displaces the theorization of the cinema as the, largely unconscious, central mode for understanding the moving image. An analysis of the cinema must posit its object as one mode of the moving image among others.

Even aesthetic thought about the cinema stands to benefit from a more broadly based understanding of the potential of film and video. Motion picture media cannot be understood in isolation, their essences cannot be derived from the technical capacity of the media at a particular historical movement as early theorists, such as Hugo Münsterberg and Rudolf Arnheim attempted to do. Motion picture media can only be comprehended together with the modes of thought and life that develop through and alongside them. The juridical use of moving images offers a very useful case for such a study since some of the thought organizing the images and governing their use is recorded in the form of case law, or appeals court decisions.

In the chapters that follow I read a series of appeals court decisions setting the precedents determining whether and how films and videos could be used in court. These decisions, known as case law, offer a record of the reasoning behind the rulemaking process. I take the chain of precedent as the record of an institution's motion picture practices. In addition to case law, I read policy statements, production manuals for attorneys, as well as journalists' accounts of evidentiary films and videos. This corpus records the heterogeneous uses the legal community has found for motion pictures and articulates the way their practices have changed over time.

2

Introducing Films into the Courts
The 1920s

As of the early 1920s, lawyers had not commonly presented films as evidence in United States courts, although motion picture technology and a precedent allowing the use of evidentiary photographs had been available since the nineteenth century. A twenty-first-century reader might be surprised at the absence of evidentiary films in early twentieth-century U.S. courts since contemporary courts routinely consider video evidence. Videos have been central to famous cases, such as the first prosecution of the police officers who beat Rodney King (1993) and the murder trial of O. J. Simpson (1997). Today, we consult video so frequently that it seems implausible to imagine a time when judges resisted admitting films into evidence. Countless images, ranging from broadcast news to scientific recordings and home movies, transmit and preserve what was once ephemeral. Those pictures confirm the transparency of film and video, they make the use of video evidence seem obvious and natural. The presentation of film and video evidence in court conforms to both our general cultural assumptions and more specialized theories of media. The slow and difficult integration of films into trials marks the slow emergence of our era from the previous one, when the relationship between images and truth was very different.

It took fifteen years, between 1920 and 1935, for federal and state courts to develop a firm precedent allowing films to be admitted into evidence. Until the 1920s, judges associated motion pictures with spectacle and chicanery, resisting their introduction into the legal system. Judges hesitate to accept new techniques and practices in legal proceedings for fear of being overturned by an appeals court, and as a consequence, establishing precedent tends to be a slow process. Before 1920, courts had adjudicated many copyright suits involving commercial films, but the films were not shown at trial. Instead, juries heard the testimony of witnesses who had seen the images.

Pressure to admit films into evidence came from attorneys' eagerness to experiment with novel ways to sway a jury. They sought to show evidentiary films before judges established a precedent for their use; if a trial judge ruled a film inadmissible, lawyers used that ruling as grounds for appeal. Consequently, judges could be found in error for excluding films as well as for admitting them. Eventually, judges responded to lawyers' attempts to present evidentiary films by defining the moving image, establishing the conditions under which it could be entered into evidence, determining what sorts of inferences might be drawn from it, and developing protocols for its projection. All of this had to be framed within the already delimited categories of admissible evidence. That process created a type of moving image particular to the juridical institution and allowed a new technology to be used in court.

In the early part of the twentieth century, jurists worried that films could convince a jury without being proved accurate. They resisted admitting films into evidence until a protocol was developed to ensure the truth of what a film showed. At first, judges invoked characteristics of film as a medium to argue for excluding it. Later, they grounded their arguments for what films allow a spectator to *know*, not what film *is*. Judges moved from *ontological* concerns about film to *epistemological* considerations.

The courts were concerned about the unusual persuasiveness of films, that juries would uncritically take the images on screen for facts that "speak for themselves," and that motion pictures would arrest the flow of speech used to establish the truth at trial. The courts understood evidentiary films as giving a clearer understanding of physical facts than does testimony but required that witnesses testify as to the accuracy of a film presented as evidence. This conception turned the image into an illustration of the speech that guarantees its veracity. By attempting to give film an illustrative rather than a probative role and by grounding the truthfulness of a film in the testimony of the witness authenticating it, the courts tried to screen out any unjustified persuasive force in motion pictures by contextualizing the image in the flow of speech. This conception of film, one particular to the courts and different from the conception of film at work in the cinema or medicine, made the projection of motion pictures in courts possible. The development of a precedent allowing the courts to use film as evidence can best be exposed by an analysis of the appellate court decisions setting the precedent allowing its use, notes from law journals, treatises on evidence, and articles in a film trade publication. These writings cite one another and articulate the first frame within which filmed evidence could be presented in court. Furthermore, they give us a series of statements that transform one another according to implicit and explicit rules, and, in so doing, govern the trial process. These texts might be thought of as a regulative and regulated discourse. Early appellate decisions, also known as case law, often found the exclusion of a film from evidence to be proper. The following analysis of the decision in *Feeny v. Young*, the earliest appellate court ruling on evidentiary film, illustrates judicial resistance to its use. After the reading of *Feeny*, an examination of the language of early case law shows that it expresses the courts' lack of familiarity with film. Next comes the presentation of a pair of cases that created a space within which to project motion pictures as evidence, despite the concerns of jurists. A series of dovetailed articles in which we find judges and lawyers attempting to control the persuasive force of films provides the following step in the exposition. Finally, a commentary on cases from early 1932 to 1937, in which the courts found themselves increasingly unable to govern the use of motion picture evidence with a unified set of principles, indicates the conceptual challenges that faced the courts after they had defined film in such a way that it could be used as evidence.

Before the Frame: Excluding Films

The earliest appellate court rulings on evidentiary films treated motion picture technology as an alien, disruptive element in the courtroom. Though courts had adjudicated copyright cases involving the content of commercial movies, they were unprepared to deal with reels of film and projection equipment. Materials were not the only problem, courts also had difficulty handling film's ephemeral and shadowy images. The 1920

New York Supreme Court case *Feeny v. Young* exemplifies resistance to exhibiting films in court and uncertainty as to how a motion picture could function as evidence. The early difficulties in presenting films as evidence are revealed by the reasoning that excluded the documentary film at issue in this case.

In the case, tried in the New York State courts, Katherine M. Feeny sued her obstetrician John Van Doren Young for publicly exhibiting images of her cesarean section in a movie entitled *Birth*. Feeny had given Young permission to film her cesarean section for the purpose of showing it to medical schools in the "interest of science" (482) but Young had not told her that he intended to circulate the film in commercial cinemas. Young had the footage edited together with images of other deliveries, and the resulting film played at "two of the leading moving picture houses in New York" (482). In order to prove that Young had violated his agreement with her, Feeny had to show that *Birth* in fact contained images of her operation.

The trial judge would not allow the film to be shown in court for purposes of identifying Feeny. He did not know how a movie could be shown so as to conform with established evidentiary practice. The appellate court agreed, opining that although the film reels themselves had been present in court, "the picture naturally could not there be thrown on the screen" (482). Projecting a film in court was almost unthinkable at this time; it would have not been "natural." The scenes from *Birth* in which Feeny appeared were excluded not because the judge thought that they might prejudice the jury or because he deemed them too shocking, but because the court did not know to deal with projection, a practice for which no precedent had been established. The court did not allow the images into evidence because they *were* a film, excluding them on ontological grounds.

Judge Smith, the appellate judge in the case, found it self-evident that a motion picture could not be shown at trial. He was particularly concerned by the ephemeral character of the film image. He wrote that while a still photograph could be used as evidence, the images on film stock itself were too small to be intelligible, and projected films produced "a flash picture, presented only for a moment" (482). He rejected the possibility of using films at trial because of the brevity of their presence on screen. The temporality of the "flash picture" is neither that of the discourse of a witness present in court, who may be cross-examined, nor that of a photograph whose image can remain the same for the duration of a trial.

That Smith considered the examination of the unprojected print as a possible means of presenting *Birth* as evidence, together with his unwillingness to allow a screening because of the fleeting charter of "flash pictures," attests to the court's unfamiliarity with film. Instead of conceptualizing the film as a continuous motion picture, the judge could only see it as a series of still images, each replacing the other on the screen. When Smith considered the film's admissibility on the basis of the precedent allowing the admission of photographs, the judge assumed that the printed quasi-permanence of the still picture functioned as criterion for the admissibility of filmed evidence. He reasoned as if the precedent of photographic evidence required that evidentiary films have the materiality of photographs to be admitted. Eventually, the admissibility of photographs provided the argument for the admission of films, on the basis of the way in which they were produced and their protocols of authentication.

Given the court's unwillingness to screen *Birth*, Feeny sought to prove that it contained images of her giving birth through the testimony of witnesses who had seen the film. Although attorneys had commonly used that technique in copyright cases involving films, Young objected that such testimony did not constitute the "best evidence." The best evidence rule states that courts must prefer the original of a document to a copy when the original exists. The trial court sustained his objection, ruling that the film itself, although it could not be screened in court, was the best evidence of what it showed.

The appellate court found that the trial court's ruling was in error and that eyewitness testimony constituted the best evidence about what the film showed. Smith cited a digest of case law concerning the film industry in Britain and America called *The Law of Motion Pictures* as an authority on this issue. The section cited by Smith states that in cases involving copyright violations, the parties wishing to prove the contents of a film must call witnesses to describe the film.

The protocol described in *The Law of Motion Pictures* allowed courts to adjudicate cases involving films while keeping the motion pictures themselves outside the juridical institution. Testimony about content of films could be entered into evidence in the same way as testimony about any other fact at issue. There was, however, no precedent for the use of film in court.

Admitting Film, Excluding Films: An
Implicit Frame

Soon after *Feeny v. Young,* courts began to admit films as evidence in a variety of cases even as they continued to show distaste for moving images. They began allowing films to appear at trial while at the same time limiting their uses and protecting their right to exclude films, as in the case of *Gibson v. Gunn.* In 1923, William H. Gibson, a vaudevillian with an amputated foot, sued Basil H. Gunn in New York State courts for injuries sustained in an auto accident. Before the accident, the defendant's foot had been cut off five inches above the ankle as a result of a previous accident, despite which Gibson continued to work as a dancer using a prosthetic foot. Gibson claimed that the injuries he sustained in his accident with Gunn ended his career.

In order to show the jury his skills as they had existed in the period between his amputation and the car accident, Gibson offered into evidence a film of himself that he had shot as a prelude to his performances. According to the appeals court, the movie began with a poem printed on a title card and then cut to a shot of Gibson walking down the street on crutches and stopping in front of a window display of artificial limbs. Gibson was next seen entering the shop and then leaving, walking down the stairs and along the street without aid. In the following scene, he met two dancers of his acquaintance who performed some steps, whereupon Gibson imitated them. At the end of the film, Gibson showed the others some steps that were too difficult for the other dancers to copy (*Gibson v. Gunn*) (20).

Gunn appealed the trial court's verdict in favor of Gibson on the grounds that the film had been erroneously entered into evidence over his objections and that it had prejudiced the jury. The appellate court held that the introduction of this film constituted reversible error. In a *per curium* opinion, the New York Supreme Court wrote:

> Aside from the fact that moving pictures present a fertile field for exaggeration of any emotion or action, and the lack of any evidence as to how this particular film was prepared, we think the picture admitted in evidence brought before the jury irrelevant matter, hearsay, and incompetent evidence which tended to make a farce of the trial. (*Gibson v. Gunn*) (20)

The court had four concerns about the use of film in this case:

1. It was wary of the potential distortion inherent in films: the possibility that physical movements could be altered as well as film's tendency to heighten emotions.
2. The court was also concerned that Gibson had not laid a foundation for the film. While a protocol for authenticating motion pictures had yet to be developed, it was already clear that, like any other form of evidence, it was necessary to show that films were what they purported to be. While it is likely that Gibson testified that the film was an accurate representation of his former abilities as a vaudevillian, the appellate court felt the need for some testimony about the production of the film. This requirement corresponded to the suspicious attitude toward motion pictures in general. Since the court felt that films were "a fertile field for exaggeration," it required that some technical proof of their accuracy should be presented. The opinion implies that it is necessary to give an account of any particular film's validity as a recording. The court framed film as a form of evidence likely to be erroneously seen as physical proof and attempted to ground that appearance in testimony.
3. The court also argued that the film should have been excluded as hearsay: testimony about statements made outside of court as if the film were an illustration of statements made elsewhere than at the trial.
4. Finally, the court ruled that the film presented much that was irrelevant to the case, a matter no doubt linked to the fact that the film in question was made as a form of entertainment. It included a poem and a formed narrative of Gibson overcoming injury rather than merely showing his ability to dance with a prosthesis. Gibson's film not only depicted him dancing but it did so in a such a way as to portray his ability as a triumph, which fueled the court's suspicion about film's exaggeration of emotion.

Gibson's former ability to dance is relevant to the case nonetheless, as it addresses the issue of the effect of his injury on his career. However, the film contained irrelevant narrative and emotional elements that might have prejudiced the jury. Those components might have garnered the jury's sympathy for Gibson. The court also attributed to the film the power to undermine the seriousness of the trial and turn it into a farce. Instead of a motion picture framed in the juridical context, the court saw the film in *Gibson v. Gunn* as transforming the courtroom as vaudeville theater.

The opinion in *Gibson v. Gunn* remains suspicious of evidentiary film, but it does not require the exclusion of all films *because they are films*. It held that the specific film offered in the case was not admissible because of what it did and did not allow the jury to *know* and what was and was not made known about the film itself. The opinion implies that judges might properly admit some motion pictures so long as the courts can be secured against films' tendency toward physical and emotional exaggeration, the films are properly authenticated, and shown to be relevant.

With these implicit criteria, *Gibson v. Gunn* framed evidentiary film as a form of physical proof of the events depicted. The opinion's concern about the "preparation" of the film shows that the court wanted assurances that the film depicted events that had unfolded in front of the camera, calling for knowledge about how the film was made. The need to guarantee the relationship between the image and truth guided courts. For something to be true in court, the evidence supporting it must be shown to be what it purports to be, and that can only be established by knowledge about the evidence usually in the form of testimony, never in the object itself. In addition, parties may only offer evidence as part of a reasoned argument rather than an emotional appeal. Although the court in *Gibson v. Gunn* does not explicitly show how a film might meet those requirements, in directing its critique against the particular film offered by Gibson rather than against motion pictures in general, it implies that courts might correctly admit certain films as evidence.

Even as jurists developed a framework for admitting films, they protected their power to exclude films. The 1926 case of *DeCamp v. United States* illustrates how the courts continued to permit the possibility of entering films into evidence while excluding specific films. The appellate court's opinion rules on the films in the case while developing a theory of evidentiary film whereby the film itself need not constitute physical proof, a very different theory from the one implied in *Gibson v. Gunn*. In *DeCamp v. United States*, the federal government prosecuted James DeCamp for fraudulently using the mails to sell stock in the Crystal Glass Casket Company, a company purporting to make glass funeral caskets, which the government argued could not be manufactured in an economically feasible manner. To show that it produced such caskets, the defendant offered a movie showing his plant in operation and asked the court for permission to project it. The trial judged denied DeCamp's request and excluded the evidence, a ruling that DeCamp cited as error on appeal.

The appellate court upheld the trial court's decision, ruling that "a motion picture does not in itself prove an actual occurrence. The thing reproduced must be established by testimony of witnesses" (*DeCamp v. United States*) (985). The appellate judge, Josiah A. Van Orsdale, wanted what the film depicted to be authenticated by testimony, though not necessarily testimony about how the film had been made. His finding called for the testimony of an eyewitness to the "occurrence" depicted in the film. His opinion makes the admission of evidentiary film dependent on the probative value of testimony. Such a perspective on motion picture evidence would develop in opposition to that which sees films as physical evidence, as in *Gibson v. Gunn*. Van Orsdale supported his reasoning with an extensive quotation from Wigmore's treatise on evidence. However, the court further ruled that the testimony about the production of the caskets presented on behalf of the defendant gave the trial court grounds to exclude the film as cumulative evidence, only showing facts already in evidence:

> If, as contended by council for the appellant, the testimony relative to the process of manufacture completely verifies the picture, then he cannot successfully claim injury from the refusal of the court to repeat this testimony to the jury by a moving picture display of the facts already in evidence. This is not the case of a photograph used to show the relative position of different objects, or to reconcile disputed issues of fact. The proofs as to conditions of manufacture at the Oklahoma plant were testified to by witnesses presumed to be familiar with existing conditions; hence the admission of the motion pictures would have amounted to a spectacular display of a situation based on facts in evidence. (*DeCamp v. United States*, 1926) (985)

Van Orsdale ruled that the film was properly excluded because "the spectacular display of a situation based on facts already in evidence" adds nothing to the jury's understanding of the case. The opinion shows the potential paradox in treating films as illustrations of testimony: in order for them to be admitted into evidence, a witness must present testimony about its contents, but testimony proving the films' contents tends to make the films cumulative evidence. The judge's argument that the testimony about the contents of the film makes the film itself redundant and hence inadmissible leads him to the conclusion that when an evidentiary film is not being used to clarify spatial or temporal relationships, it has no advantage over testimony and that, in this case, the defense wanted to show the film in order to mislead the jury into thinking that seeing a film is tantamount to seeing the actual events. His decision equates the probative value of a film with the probative value of testimony and accords it only a clarifying function. Like the opinion in *Gibson v. Gunn*, Van Orsdale's opinion is wary of film's potential surplus of persuasive force and seeks to preserve a judge's authority to exclude films.

Installing the Apparatus: Film as Foreign Body

Although courts would soon set a definitive, positively stated precedent allowing the projection of films at trial, jurists would write about motion pictures as a foreign importation into courtrooms for almost twenty years after the decision in *Feeny v. Young*. The case law from the 1920s and 1930s often manifested a certain resistance to the use of evidentiary films as exemplified in the 1928 decision in *Massachusetts Bonding & Ins. Co. v. Worthy*, written by Judge Hodges of the Texas State Court of Appeals. A painter named Worthy who worked for the Cotton Belt Railroad fell twenty-three feet from a scaffolding and fractured his sacrum. Worthy testified that his injuries were so severe he could not hold down jobs he had started *after* the accident at a restaurant and as a meat cutter. The insurance company refused to pay on the grounds that, contrary to his claim, Worthy was not completely incapacitated. Two doctors testified for Worthy as to the severity of his fracture, but the trial court did not allow the defense to impeach their testimony by introducing images of the plaintiff in action "such as are commonly called 'motion pictures'" (*Massachusetts Bonding & Ins. Co. v. Worthy*, 1928) (393). The judge's language here reveals his relative unfamiliarity with films as evidence and his sense of their foreignness to the judicial process.

The films purported to contradict Worthy's claim that he had been totally disabled, but the appellate court ruled that they were neither properly identified nor accurate representations. The opinion stated, "The bills of exception do not contain the pictures, nor show what they would disclose; nor did the bills of exception show how the pictures were to be shown to the jury" (393). The introduction of motion pictures remained an occasion for concern about the propriety of the projection apparatus in the courtroom as well as the possibility of tampering. The judge wrote further, "It is a matter of common knowledge that pictures showing a person in action may be made very deceptive by the operator of the machine used in taking the pictures" (393). Common knowledge about motion pictures in general here compensates for the judge's unfamiliarity with evidentiary film, and judicial reasoning based on such "common knowledge" is characteristic of decisions in this period. The opinion in *Gibson v. Gunn* also relies on *doxa* when it states that motion pictures are "a fertile field for exaggeration." Judges used *doxa* about movies in general to start thinking about evidentiary films in particular. Since *doxa* constitutes a shared set of opinions or assumptions about motion pictures, opinions also often cited commonplaces in order to communicate their judgments.

As late as 1932, *Chima v. Railroad*'s appellate court judge described an attempt to show motion picture evidence as an effort to "install in the courtroom a moving picture apparatus" (*State for use of Anna Chima*). The phrase makes it clear that everything involved in the projection of film comes from outside the courtroom and must be installed. The strangeness of film in courtrooms lingered long after the courts had begun to admit it as evidence. Its alien character came from both the novelty of the medium in the courts and from the projection apparatus that had to be grafted onto the courtroom's infrastructure when the occasion required. The decorum of trials was strictly enforced and any change in the physical disposition of the court's space was met with suspicion.

Screening the Surplus: Events and Reenactments

Jurists began to formulate explicit rules for the use of evidentiary films as attorneys increasingly sought to show evidentiary motion pictures at trial. Instead of allowing or barring evidentiary films in general, such rules pertained to specific classes of evidentiary film. In their initial attempts to devise such rules, jurists divided films into two categories: films that directly showed events at issue in a trial and films that depicted reconstructions of these events. Courts routinely admitted the former if properly authenticated but treated the latter with much more suspicion. Jurists wrote about the films directly showing events as the best form of evidence available to courts, but they feared that reconstructions introduced a bias into the representation of events.

Judge Ernst Weyand formulated the distinction between films of events and filmed reconstructions in the February 21, 1920 issue of *Moving Picture World*, a magazine for movie fans. Weyand presided over the trial of Gertrude Wilson for the murder of Charles Brown, in which the defense sought to introduce into evidence a reenactment of the murder filmed by a professional director according to a witness's testimony. Weyand screened the film without the jury present and spent half a day hearing arguments for and against the admission of the film in order to decide whether to allow its entry into evidence. The defense argued that the film showed the murder exactly as it happened and that it was the only means of describing it with such precision, contending that without it, the jurors would have to piece together twelve different mental pictures of what happened from oral testimony, whereas a film would leave each juror with one and the same impression. This argument, that a film gives the jury a single image rather than the twelve it would conjure while listening to testimony, would become one of the major claims made for the evidentiary film and video through the 1970s.

Judge Weyand excluded the film because it might unduly sway the jury "by its dramatic effect" (1257). "Dramatic effect" included at least two factors:

First, the actors' performances in the film might favor the argument of the party offering the film. Weyand noted that the actors in the film offered by Wilson were not witnesses to the murder, their performances guided only by the defense's version of event. The dramatization of the defendant's version of events seemed to Weyand to carry a powerful and dangerous persuasive force.

Second, Weyand felt that jurors tend to accept what they see in still photographs as fact even when told that the images depict a conjecture, adding that motion pictures present an even greater risk of seducing the jury into taking a version of events for facts. He excluded the film from evidence out of concern that the jury might more easily accept the defense's version as true if it were presented by means of the film than through the testimony of a witness.

The dramatic effect that concerned Weyand constitutes a surplus produced by film as a medium. This surplus lies not in anything that the film shows but in the fact that the film shows rather than tells, in something very like film's supposed power to give twelve jurors a single image of events. It would have been perfectly admissible for the defense to give its version of events as testimony. The film added to the defendant's account a seemingly factual character, and that surplus gives the film power of persuasion lacking in testimony. The opinions in *Gibson v. Gunn* and *DeCamp v. United States* considered above would seek to control this same persuasive force.

Judge Weyand very clearly explained the difference between a filmed reconstruction such as the one he had excluded and films showing the events at issue in a case. He said that motion pictures should be admitted into evidence when offered "in the aid of any disputed issue in court in an attempt to have a clear mental picture of the incident under investigation and in order to have it clearly impressed on the minds of the court and jury" (1257). Weyand believed that any exclusion of such films constituted reversible error, giving as examples a film of a mechanical device that is impractical to bring into court but whose functioning is at issue and a film being made on a street when an altercation breaks out. Weyand also imagined films recording the illegal actions of picketers during strikes, writing that such a film would be "the very best evidence" (1257). The judge emphasized that in all his examples the films show "the direct fact at issue" (1257). Weyand's assessment presciently described the use of serendipitous recordings of events as evidence, a practice that would not become common until the mass distribution of small video cameras and that was made famous in the trial of the police officers who beat Rodney King.

Weyand's distinction between films of events and filmed reconstructions of them implies that everything seen in a film appears as fact. Weyand's argument implies that film's produce their own evidentiary value, independently of the testimony that supporting them. He leaned toward the exclusion of filmed reenactments because they tend to be taken as showing facts but favored the admission of direct films because they do show facts, and so their persuasive supplement does not deceive.

Weyand stated that the film in the Wilson case would have been admissible evidence if the possibility of the murder occurring in the way shown by the film had been an issue at trial, then the film of the reenacted murder could have demonstrated that the murder *could have been* committed as claimed.

Through a network of citation that crosses genres and institutions, Weyand's concerns about film's power to persuade became part of the earliest authoritative commentary on evidentiary films. The *New York Times* of February 22, 1920 carried a piece based on the *Moving Picture World* article entitled "Movies as Evidence." John Henry Wigmore's *Treatise on The Anglo-American System of Evidence* in turn cited the article (124). Wigmore states that litigants make filmed reconstructions to persuade courts of their versions of events, and while all evidence is offered in favor of one side or the other, moving pictures are "apt to cause forgetfulness of this and to impress the jury with the convincing impartiality of Nature herself" (124). Like Weyand, Wigmore locates the bias in the reconstruction of the event at issue rather than in the way it is filmed. In his account of filmed reconstructions, the persuasive power of motion pictures works by rendering the bias of the recreation invisible. Film gives the artificial reconstruction the appearance of a natural event rather than an account of that event.

Wigmore's analysis of the naturalizing effect begins to delineate the tension between theories of evidence based on the primacy of testimony and those based on the primacy of seeing, a distinction already at work in the argument from the Wilson case that a film would give the jury a single image instead of twelve images. Wigmore's *Treatise* equates photographs with "someone's testimony" and points out that in order to be entered into evidence, still pictures must be authenticated by a witness to what they depict. Wigmore uses this point to argue that courts should admit films into evidence on the same basis as still photographs, suggesting that jurists should also treat film as testimony. Yet, if film were the same as testimony, it seems unlikely that Wigmore would be concerned about film's ability to make a jury mistake a reconstruction for a direct recording of an event. The productive tension in Wigmore's argument comes from dialectic whereby film's ability to mislead comes from its potential for neutrality. Wigmore and Weyand both classify evidentiary films according to whether they directly depict events or reconstructions of events at issue in a case. On the basis of this classification, rules governing the admissibility of moving images can be derived and very little regulation of films directly showing events is needed, but reenactment films call for great vigilance.

According to Wigmore, reenactments require care on the part of the trial court because the question of whether a film might mislead the jury can only be decided on a case-by-case basis. This argument placed the question of the admissibility of certain films squarely within the discretion of the trial court. As the use of evidentiary films increased in the 1920s and 1930s, the contingencies of particular cases began to slow the development of general principles regulating the use of motion picture evidence. The vigilance required by reenactments made judicial improvisation a rule.

The distinction between films that capture events and films of reconstructions was an initial step in jurisprudence limiting the persuasive power of film. However, that very power made the use of evidentiary films attractive to litigants, as one can read in a note on the use of motion picture evidence that appeared in the *Illinois Law Review* in 1933. The author of this note, Herbert H. Kennedy, gives an account of a personal injury case in which he acted as counsel for the defense and offered motion pictures into evidence. After having elicited testimony from the plaintiff that between certain dates she could not walk without a limp or get about without using a cane in snowy weather, Kennedy showed films of her walking easily through four inches of snow. Kennedy wrote that "if a correct foundation for impeachment is laid and the moving pictures produced at a psychological moment, the entire value of an opponent's case may be destroyed" (Kennedy). Testimony to the effect that a witness had seen the plaintiff walking easily in bad weather would also impeach the plaintiff's testimony but would not destroy the value of her case so effectively. The case-destroying force described by Kennedy comes from the medium of film itself.

At the end of his article, Kennedy outlines a protocol for the authentication of evidentiary films that would become standard procedure in the late 1930s and early 1940s. The party offering the evidence must lay a foundation for it with testimony as to every phase of the filmmaking process: the operator, the camera and film, the exposures used, the way the film was developed, the operation of the projector, and the state of the screen—testimony that the film is a fair and accurate representation of what it shows. Kennedy presents this protocol as a means of ensuring that an evidentiary film is admitted into evidence by the judge presiding over the case by preempting as many objections to it as possible. Since Kennedy was "not aware of any decision defining what evidence is necessary to lay a foundation for the introduction of such pictures" (426), the protocol provides as much evidence as possible. Like testimony establishing a chain of custody ensuring a piece of physical evidence's integrity, the protocol's rhetoric attempts to verify every link connecting the facts the film shows to the appearance of the image on a courthouse screen.

Unlike Wigmore, Kennedy suggested foundational testimony aimed at establishing the film offered as a kind of physical proof of what it shows. This protocol not only assures the admission of a film into evidence, but it also heightens its persuasive power. By soliciting testimony showing that the film presents a scene exactly as it appeared when the film was shot, the authentication protocol frames the film as a means of letting the jury see the scene as if it was looking at it directly. Evidentiary film's potential to "destroy" testimony comes from the conviction that it adds nothing to the scenes it records. Kennedy's protocol of authentication worked to make the film more persuasive for the jury by making it more transparent and so making it more persuasive.

This power can also be seen working in early case law concerning the admission of sound films into evidence. The earliest appellate court decision concerning sound films dates from 1931. In the case of Commonwealth v. Roller, tried in the Philadelphia courts and appealed to the Pennsylvania Superior Court, police arrested Harold Roller for larceny and recorded his confession on a sound film. Over the objections of the defense, the trial court admitted the film into evidence. The defense appealed on the grounds that the admission of the film constituted reversible error.

In his opinion, Judge Robert S. Gawthorp found that motion pictures were "constantly used for commercial and scientific purposes" (Gawthorp, 1931) (127) and that the courts generally acknowledged them as admissible evidence. Previous opinions drew doxa from common knowledge about the cinema, but Roller invokes scientific uses of film to justify its use as evidence, treating the medium as a technology with multiple uses instead of taking cinema as the medium's normal and normative use. The court reasoned that the scientific community considered films valid recordings of events and that courts were thus justified in screening evidentiary films. *Roller's* argument treats sound films as a kind of physical proof, not as testimony, even if the film was of Roller confessing. The appellate court approved the reasoning of the lower court in that it admitted the sound films on the basis of precedents that admitted phonograph records and silent films.

Despite its sophistication, the opinion reveals that the judge was relatively unfamiliar with the film industry when it goes on to state that "the talking motion picture, or movietone as it is technically known, results merely from an adaptation of the scientific process used in producing photographic records, in order that the words spoken or the sounds produced at the time of the taking of the pictures may be reproduced with the picture" (Gawthorp, 1931) (127). The court's use of "movietone" as a technical term, rather than as a brand name, not only indicates the court's inexperience but also underscores the privileged position of scientific discourse in the juridical framing of films as admissible evidence with its insistence on the "technical."

Although the opinion framed talking motion pictures as a scientifically valid means of recording, it had no need to address the issue of why it would be preferable to present a filmed confession rather than a signed transcript of the confession. In *Roller*, the use of sound film instead of a written confession can only be explained by the persuasive power of the medium. There should be no difference between the probative value of a transcript and that of a film. Anything a film adds to such a document ought to be screened out by framing moving pictures as a means of recording; yet, from a pragmatic standpoint, litigants use motion pictures to present confessions because they think the films will be more convincing than a transcript.

Wigmore and Weyand's attempts to regulate the use of evidentiary films according to a set of general principles set the example for this period. Lawyers had not yet offered evidentiary films in great enough quantities for justices to understand that there were many categories beyond films of facts at issue and reenactments. As a result of their creativity, motion pictures would no longer be treated as a single class of evidence governed by a single set of rules. The lack of general rules of admissibility for motion picture evidence was a consequence of the fact that legal institution's need to apply rules and concepts to historical situations developing contingently. Evidentiary law developed as a series of responses to new forms of evidence lawyers attempted to use in trials.

As the applications of motion pictures in courts changed, the rules governing their use passed from the general to the particular so that the rules in question governed an ever-decreasing portion of evidentiary films. As the applications of evidentiary films multiplied, case law increasingly tended to rely on the discretion of the trial courts to settle matters of admissibility for all kinds of films. This discretion required justices to improvise rather than requiring them to use a rule established by a precedent.

Tracing the Frame's Work

Chima v. Railroad firmly established the trial court's discretionary power in admitting particular films, and the opinion indicates that no single set of rules can govern the use of evidentiary films. This federal case concerned Anna Chima's son, Theodore B. Dan, who died in a streetcar accident. She claimed that the swaying of the car had caused him to receive a fatal blow on the head. The trolley company claimed that he had ill-advisedly stuck his head out the window to greet a friend in a passing car. The trial court decided in favor of the defendant.

The plaintiff had offered into evidence a film of a streetcar going around the turn where the accident had occurred. The film did not show the accident itself but rather a filmed reconstruction of a different car made after the accident. The film supposedly demonstrated that all cars swayed at the point on the track where the accident occurred, but to prove her case, the plaintiff would have had to show that the swaying had been "unusual or extraordinary" enough to cause Chima's son's death. Judge Dennis of the Maryland Supreme Court wrote that it seemed improbable that the extraordinary force involved in the accident could be shown using another car. He pointed out that the car in the moving picture might have traveled at a faster rate and thus swayed more than the car in the accident and that the film might have been shot so as to exaggerate the speed of the trolley. The opinion mentions concerns about the validity of experiments as evidence in court as well as those about the fidelity of moving images. By linking the admission of films to the admissibility of the experiments depicted therein, *Chima v. Railroad* opened a new avenue of dispersal for the rules governing motion picture evidence. Dennis treated the film not as a reconstruction but as the means for presenting an experiment to the courts, acknowledging that the film functioned as a different class of evidence governed by a distinct set of rules.

Chima v. Railroad also addressed issues that applied to all evidentiary films in order to establish the authority of trial courts in admitting evidentiary films. Dennis acknowledged the importance of questions about convenience and confusion in the courtroom in deciding whether to admit a film and invoked these factors to support his argument that evidentiary films could not be subjected to a single set of rules. Because the admissibility of films varies from case to case, and the rules governing various classes of evidence change, he wrote that the question "must largely be left to the discretion of the presiding judge without any restricting general formula laid down to control him" (*Chima v. Railroad*) (418).

The uneven development of case law in the various state court systems encouraged the broad discretionary powers of trial courts in admitting evidentiary films. In some states, the issues presented by the use of filmed reenactments and filmed experiments continued to be of special concern to the courts throughout the 1930s. A Mississippi case, *Gulf Life v. Stossel,* confronted the courts with the issues involved in filmed recreations as late as 1938. *Stossel* concerned a boating accident. One of the parties offered a film reconstructing the accident. The opposing party objected to the film on the grounds that it had been made by one of the litigants without the presence of the other party. This objection addressed the concerns about filmed recreations that had arisen with Weyand's ruling in the Wilson case. The court reasoned that by having both parties present at the filming of the reconstruction along with a commissioner, the bias in the reconstruction might be avoided. It ruled that the trial court must appoint a commissioner in cases involving such films, and that the other party should be given the opportunity to be present.

When neither litigant felt that a commissioner was needed, the film was admissible so long as it was properly authenticated and shown to be a faithful representation of the subject. The opinion left open this question of fidelity as a matter for testimony rather than something guaranteed by the technical assurances made possible by a supervised production process. One of the members of the Supreme Court, Justice Brown, expressed concern about the time constraints imposed on the production of motion picture evidence by the procedure suggested. Brown pointed out that "there might be cases where such pictures taken before the controversy gets into court would be valuable evidence" (*Gulf Life v. Stossel*) (270). He held that only pictures taken after a case had already started needed to be shot under the supervision of a commissioner.

Judge Brown wrote that films should be admitted under the rules that govern the admission of photographs since "after all, moving pictures are nothing but a rapidly taken series of still pictures" (128). The precedent establishing the admissibility of evidentiary photographs gave trial judges broad discretionary powers in ruling on whether to admit a particular piece of evidence and, by grounding the admissibility of films on the precedent of photographs, Brown evoked another model in which judicial improvisation displaced rules. That displacement allowed the courts to deal with media used by litigants to present various types of evidence.

While courts found that they could not govern the use of evidentiary films with a single set of rules, they remained concerned about the reliability of film in general. Jurists addressed this by requiring a foundation of testimony to contain evidentiary film's persuasive power. A 1934 opinion by Judge Francis Martin of the New York Supreme Court in the case of *Boyarski v. Zimmerman* represented the next stage in the development of case law, when the courts commonly treated films as more probative than testimony. Martin's decision was cited in case law as late as the 1980s and is as close to a controlling case as exists concerning the question of motion picture evidence. The only rule it establishes is negative, holding that courts cannot exclude films from evidence merely because they were films.

Boyarski brought a personal injury suit against the G. A. Zimmerman company, for whom he had worked under a subcontractor as a plumber's helper building the Hollywood Theater in New York City. According to his testimony, while Boyarski worked in the basement, a bolt from beams being riveted thirty feet above hit him on the head, a blow that he claimed rendered him unable to do work of any kind. Unbeknownst to the plaintiff, the defense had shot a film of him walking down the road carrying a package in Bridgeport, Connecticut. The defense offered it into evidence as proof that Boyarski had exaggerated the severity of his injuries.

The trial court did not admit these films into evidence and, on appeal, Zimmerman cited their exclusion as error. Zimmerman noted that the New York State Supreme Court and federal courts had admitted films into evidence (*Boyarski v. Zimmerman*) (138). Using the same logic as Judge Brown in *Gulf v. Stossel*, the defense argued for admissibility of films in general, contending that if still pictures are admissible, there is no reason why motion pictures should not be.

In his opinion, Judge Martin noted that New York courts held "very decided and divergent views" about the admissibility of motion picture evidence (*Boyarski v. Zimmerman*) (137) and had not decisively settled the matter of their admissibility before this case. According to Martin, the films offered by Zimmerman were "not only admissible but very important" (138) in assessing Boyarski's claim of total disability. Martin found Boyarski's testimony suspect because of his interest in the verdict. The judge also mistrusted the statements of Boyarski's main witness, the subcontractor who employed him but who did not provide worker's compensation insurance. Martin believed that a film of the defendant was a more reliable form of evidence than the testimony of these interested parties. Although the defense had something at stake in the case as well, they could establish the film's fairness and accuracy.

The opinion emphasized the importance of laying a proper foundation for evidentiary films without making the conditions of that foundation explicit. Martin wrote that courts should exclude even properly authenticated motion pictures if they delay a trial, or if they merely render sensational facts that might be otherwise offered. He ruled that the judge should have allowed the jury to see pictures of Boyarski "conducting himself as a perfectly well man" (138) so that they could make up their minds about his claims. Although Boyarski's testimony as to his injury was authenticated by the oath he took on the witness stand and the films had to be authenticated by testimony, which was itself also authenticated by the same oath, the film seemed to Martin to be more probative than Boyarski's statements. Here we find a paradoxical result of the tension between the appeal of film's persuasive power for litigants and the court's need to minimize that power: films could be seen as more probative than testimony, yet they had to be authenticated by testimony, the veracity of which was established in the same way as that of all other testimony.

Martin's opinion also provides general consideration of evidentiary films. Citing "the well known progress being made in the motion picture world" in accurately presenting events, the judge indicated that the courts might benefit from using a new, generally accepted technology. He did not, however, use a scientific argument as in *Roller*, but instead referred to something presumably well known, relying on *doxa*, or *ethymemes*, as the opinion in *Gunn* did. Martin wrote, "In many cases the picture may not only have a bearing on the facts but may be absolutely decisive of the issues involved in the action" (138). Martin assumed that proper authentication can establish the truth of a film, but he did not worry about the problem of the veracity of the testimony that provides the foundation for an evidentiary film. Instead, he presented the properly authenticated motion picture as a more reliable form of evidence than testimony. The brevity with which the opinion considered the details of authentication supports this view of evidentiary films. Martin's faith in the truth of films shows itself as an effect of the same power that initially concerned Judge Weyand and attracted attorneys like Kennedy. Martin does not locate the ability of motion pictures to disclose relevant information to juries in any of the technical features of the medium; instead, he attributes it to film as representation, citing newsreels as an example of the accuracy bestowed by motion pictures. However, he does not explain why he considers newsreels to be veridical or what guarantees their truth.

The court considered trials that had properly excluded films, naming *Gibson v. Gunn* among them. The judge noted that the picture might be particularly irrelevant "if a dialogue or conversation were permitted at the time the moving picture is shown" (139), implying that films ought to speak for themselves and not be analyzed by testimony while they were being projected. In considering *Massachusetts Bonding v. Worthy*, the court again emphasized the importance of foundational testimony, arguing that "if there is any exaggeration, it may be pointed out by the court or the moving picture wholly rejected" (139).

Martin's history of the case law concerning the use of evidentiary films reveals that the varieties of motion picture evidence had proliferated beyond what could be controlled by a single set of rules, despite the New York courts not yet having established the admissibility of film in principle by 1934. Martin's opinion enlarged the scope of Wigmore's finding (cited by Martin in *Boyarski v. Zimmerman*) that "no general rule can be laid down as to the kinds of occurrences artificially reconstructed in which the motion picture would have a special risk of misleading," (108).

Pressure exerted by novel techniques gradually dissolved rules that could be applied to every evidentiary film, a process eventually resulting in a set of parameters within the boundaries of which trial judges had to improvise when adjudicating films and videos.

Doxa: The Edge of the Frame

Common opinion about the film industry's progress in producing accurate representations of events plays an important part in Martin's decision to admit the film in *Boyarski v. Zimmerman*. Martin's reasoning regarding the "well known progress" in motion pictures seems to update the *Gibson v. Gunn* ruling and to supersede the suspicion that film is "fertile field for exaggeration." Though the decision in *Zimmerman* offers a detailed reading of previous case law and mounts a powerful argument for the admissibility of properly authenticated evidentiary films, not all judges followed Martin's line of reasoning, As we have seen, some judges referred to *doxa* about the moving image to call film's usefulness as a form of evidence into question.

In an opinion written only three years after *Boyarski v. Zimmerman*, a reference to well-known developments in the cinema cautioned against admitting films into evidence too easily. In the case of *Owens v. Hegenbeck-Wallace Shows*, Buck Owens sued Hegenbeck-Wallace for breach of contract. A circus company in Peru, Indiana, hired Owens, his wife, and their trained horse in February for the whole of 1934. After a show in Boston on June 30, Owens received notice that their contract, which was to run through November 15, had been terminated because their act was no longer satisfactory to the management. Hegenbeck-Wallace also claimed that Owens had falsely asserted that his horse had appeared in various films. In order to refute this claim, Owens showed one of these films in court to counter those accusations. Hegenbeck-Wallace lost the case and appealed the film's admission as reversible error.

Later, an appellate judge called the courtroom screening an "unusual procedure" that "should be resorted to, if at all, with extreme caution" (*Owens v. Hegenbeck-Wallace*) (161). The judge stressed the necessity of proper authentication and of showing the trial judge that the film is a "true reproduction." He argued that "because of the skill and development in the fabrication of moving pictures and the possibilities of producing desired effects by cutting and other devices, a jury might receive misleading and prejudicial impressions as to important issues in a case" (161). Here, the judge uses same general knowledge about technical advances in the movies as the *Boyarski* opinion to make the very opposite point. These concerns seem largely irrelevant to *Hegenbeck-Wallace* since the film was offered to prove that Owens's horse appeared in it. Despite his general concerns, the appellate judge found that, in the present case, the defendant took no exception to the trial judge's ruling at the time of the trial and so could not appeal on the grounds that the trial court had committed reversible error. In fact, the defense attorney in the case said, "I do not wish to deprive the jury of the opportunity of viewing a movie" (161). The defense's failure to object settled the matter, since a piece of evidence cannot be found to have been admitted in error unless it is objected to when it is offered at trial.

By definition, evidentiary films must have some relationship to truth and the opinions in *Gibson v. Gunn, Boyarski v. Zimmerman,* and *Owens v. Hegenbeck-Wallace Shows* all invoke *doxa* to posit such a relationship. Evidence must have a determined position within a scheme that distinguishes between truth and appearance. If the image is found to be on the side of truth, it is admissible; if it is found to be on the side of mere appearance, it must be excluded.

In the cinema, films can assume an implicit position with regard to the truth, and in court the truth of testimony is guaranteed by the oath taken by the witnesses and by cross-examination, but evidentiary films require an explicit relation to the truth articulated by testimony outside the images themselves. In the cinema, a documentary's accuracy receives an implicit guarantee from its position in that institution. The courts require an explicit guarantee that determines the relevant, visible, and audible components of the image and makes the image evidence of something in particular. *Doxa* gave judges a point in their discourse from which to begin writing about films and their relations to truth. They began with what was generally believed about film, sometimes presenting motion pictures as accurate and other times casting doubt on the medium. The contradictory uses of commonplaces about film set in motion the courts variable framings of the moving image. The opposed arguments not only gave grounds for opposed construals of the medium of film as such, they also foreshadowed the means for affirming or calling into question any particular film.

The juridical framework consists of an agonistic polylogue involving at a minimum the two opposing parties, the judges of the trial courts, and the appellate courts. The contradictory uses of *doxa* and the adversarial structure of trials pragmatically produce the semiotic structures of evidentiary film. Those structures constantly shifted so that film appeared as scientific proof in some contexts and as pictorial testimony in others. This variation in framing involves a shift away from reasoning on the basis of general knowledge without losing the division set up by such arguments.

In this period, courts commonly construed film both as the source of accurate reproductions and as a potentially deceptive image. The evidentiary protocol suggested in Kennedy's note on motion picture evidence displaced both positions through its attempts to prove that the specific process used to produce a particular motion picture guaranteed the link between a film and what it shows. Like the arguments from *doxa*, Kennedy's reasoning assumes that the truth is something outside both the juridical process and the film, rather than something produced by adjudicating the film.

Litigants authenticated evidentiary films through eyewitness testimony that the image in question constituted a fair and accurate representation of what it showed. Such testimony gave the motion picture entered into evidence the same guarantee of truth as an oral account. One of the first cases to call explicitly for testimony about the accuracy of the representation instead of extensive technical testimony was in 1937, in *Heiman v. Railroad*. A trolley car hit Josephine Heiman and she claimed damages (extreme shock and the like), testifying that her injuries had made her "a physical and nervous wreck" (*Heiman et al. v. Market St. RY. Co.*) (179). The defendant attempted to show that she had exaggerated the extent of her injuries. Their council argued that on the day of the accident she was "going through the period of change of life" (179) and that she had received serious injuries in a previous auto accident.

Heiman claimed to have been "a confirmed invalid" during her recovery period, but the defendant introduced moving pictures that "purported to show" Heiman "driving an automobile in and out of heavy traffic; and to show her shopping, walking, stooping and bending without assistance from anyone. They also showed her carrying grocery bundles" (179).

Heiman's counsel said that no foundation had been laid but did not show what was lacking in the authentication of the film. The attorney also stated that in no instance should motion pictures be admitted into evidence because of "pranks and tricks" that can be played with them. The appellate court invalidated Heiman's objection on the grounds that the plaintiff's testimony that the films were "a true representation of the scene as witnessed by the photographer" (180) constituted a proper foundation. Instead of framing the films as scientific proof of an event, the court construed them as an accurate representation of what a witness saw.

The note from the *Illinois Law Review* of 1933 (Kennedy) had already described such a use of motion picture evidence to show malingering. As we will see in the following chapter, the courts' concern with the persuasive power of such films would soon become as great as its concerns about it in filmed recreations. Although litigants presented malingering films as if they proved that the injuries were not as severe as the plaintiffs claimed, these did not necessarily prove anything in and of themselves. Questions arose about how often the plaintiff was able to perform the actions shown on the films and whether her ability to do certain things actually were often required to disprove the claim of disability.

Conclusion

In many early cases, one of the parties appealed the verdict on the grounds that films should not be admitted into evidence at all. As the use of motion pictures in court proliferated, litigants began to object to the admission of specific films entered into evidence that lacked proper authentication or without any demonstration of their relevance to the case. The courts' attention shifted from the question of how to authenticate moving images in general to what a particular mode of authentication allows a film to prove.

The principle allowing motion pictures to be presented as evidence could not be developed into a set of rules governing their use because, although the courts treated film as a single technology, lawyers used them in a variety of legal maneuvers that generated multiple already existing classes of evidence, each of which the courts regulated with different protocols. The proliferation of classes of motion picture evidence was, as we have seen, at first driven by the persuasive surplus and the *doxa* about film in the culture at large.

Although courts attempted to frame evidentiary films so that they could not exert an unusual persuasive power on juries, the possibility of using such a power made evidentiary films attractive to attorneys, who persisted in finding ways to enter films into evidence in such a way as to maximize their persuasive effect. The courts' attempts to screen out films became a means of generating an even stronger effect because attempts to reduce the power of films actually produce and naturalize it. The less rhetorical an evidentiary film seems, the greater its persuasive force. Thus the courts' framing of films created surplus rhetorical value in the films by its very attempts to eliminate such a surplus. The greater the proof of a film's authenticity and objectivity, the more it acquires what Wigmore called "the convincing impartiality of Nature." The creation of multiple framings for evidentiary films both over time and for their use as different classes of evidence made it impossible to regulate the use of motion pictures by a stable code of rules. In the next chapter we will see what effects this variable framework had on the philosophical foundations of jurisprudence.

3

The Development of Case Law Governing the Use of Motion Picture Evidence in the 1940s and 1950s

By 1940, United States courts had established ways of working with film as an evidentiary medium, but its significance was still contested. Some films functioned as proof and others as accounts. The kind of argument used to authenticate and show the relevance of a film, to lay its foundation, presented it either as pictorial testimony or physical corroboration. According to one argument, a film constituted physical proof of what they depicted. Another argument held that a film illustrated witness testimony. The foundation laid for a film determined not only whether a film could be shown in court, but also what the court considered the film to *be*, in other words, such arguments had *ontological* effects.

The most powerful foundation for films offered them into evidence as incontrovertible proof of a point at issue in a case. Similar to an index as defined by the philosopher C. S. Peirce, such films become a representation that refers to its object "because it is in dynamical (including spatial) connection both with the individual object, on the one hand, and with the senses or memory of the person for whom it is a sign, on the other hand" (Peirce, 107). Pierce's definition includes an *epistemological* condition, concerning *knowledge* about the index and an *ontological* condition concerning what the index *is*. The person for whom it is a sign must know the index through the senses, while the index connected to which it refers. Jurists sometimes understood an evidentiary film as the result of a physical reaction that can only be produced in the presence of whatever was before the lens, fulfilling the ontological aspect of Peirce's definition.

Although evidentiary films had no connection with the jury's memory, the epistemological condition of Peirce's definition was met by the connection with the memory of the authenticating witness who authenticates them and whose testimony communicates that memory to the jury. When the image was produced, where it was produced, and what the image depicts can only be established in court through speech or writing. Only testimony guarantees the truth of evidentiary film, especially when presented as an index. The courts use the language of a third party, a witness, to present a motion picture into an index for the judge and jury, who have no perceptual or mnemonic connection to what it depicts.

Whether films were offered as proof or as illustrated testimony, their introduction was justified by an instrumental interpretation of the relationship between motion pictures and truth. In general, the party offering the films tried to present them as physical evidence while the party against whom they were offered tried to show that the films were no more necessarily truthful than the witnesses authenticating them. The first theory locates the truth of evidentiary film in seeing, the second in testimony.

This chapter analyzes the relations between evidentiary film and testimony in the 1940s and 1950s. Beginning with a brief elaboration of theories of evidence based on testimony and those based on seeing to establish a general context, it outlines the two ontological possibilities for evidentiary films by examining the increasing variety of uses attorneys put them to, a variety that brought out the contradiction between film as visual proof and film as pictorial testimony. *McGoorty v. Benhart*, where a film offered as physical proof of the plaintiff's malingering was authenticated by an inordinate amount of testimony in order to make it appear more reliable than eyewitness accounts, provides a crucial example of the effects of the foundation for entering a film. The analysis shows that in cases where films were offered as physical proof, the moving image took on the value of a sight not connected to any seer. They imparted the same image to all twelve members of the jury and brought into play the unjustified persuasiveness that jurists sought to exclude in the 1920s and 1930s.

Films used in malingering cases provide the bulk of the examples in this chapter because they reveal the rhetorical effects of films presented as an image disconnected from a seer within the adversarial structure of trials. In malingering cases, attorneys presented films to argue that plaintiffs in personal injury litigation were exaggerating their injuries. In the 1940s and 1950s, the case law controlling the use of evidentiary film during this period was developed largely in such cases. Making malingering films often involved secretly filming supposedly disabled plaintiffs who had been lured into physical activities that they claimed to be unable to perform, bringing up important matters of policy.

The Two Truths of Law

The relations between testimony and films in U.S. courts expose a latent tension in the founding assumptions of Anglo-American common law. Spoken testimony of a witness present in court, who has sworn to tell the truth, had long been considered the most reliable form of evidence, but presenting a visible object in court proves its existence. Testimony and visible evidence had each been valued as the most reliable form of evidence and they depended on one another for their effect. The presentation of physical evidence in the courtroom derives its impact from the sense that "seeing is believing." Displaying a piece of evidence in court is more convincing than any testimony *about* the existence of that piece of evidence. A gun is presented along with the testimony of a police officer that he found it at the scene of the crime because the presence of the gun to the sight of the jury is held to be a surer proof than the word of the officer alone. Yet, objects cannot speak to identify themselves, only testimony can establish what is being shown. When a piece of physical evidence is presented in court, it is only rendered intelligible on the basis of the testimony of the witness who authenticates it. A gun introduced into evidence in a murder case might be any gun; only the word of the police officer who identifies it makes it relevant to the case.

Testimony, supposedly less persuasive than visible evidence, is, in fact, required to support visible evidence. The structure is strange in that the physical, sensible evidence must function as the basis for claims that are intelligible but not directly sensible, yet the relevance and authenticity of physical evidence can only be established by the intelligibility of testimony.

The presentation of objects involved in a case, such as crime scene photos, diagrams, enlargements of fingerprints, and other exhibits, reflects the idea that truth is grounded in seeing. Such a theory is *heliocentric*—it is organized around sight, or the sensuous revelation of objects by light. Contrarily, the courts' reliance on testimony implies the living discourse of a speaker present at trial who articulates the truth. The privilege accorded to testimony implies a *phonocentric* theory whereby the truth is revealed by the voice of a witness. The heliocentric theory of truth can be aligned with a hierarchy of evidence that gives the most weight to direct perceptions, that is, to sensible evidence. The phonocentric theory of truth can be aligned with a hierarchy that gives the most weight to an understanding of events expressed in speech, that is, to an intelligible form of evidence.

Although the phonocentric and heliocentric evidentiary hierarchies seem to contradict each other, any contradiction had been held in abeyance by the courts' familiarity with most forms of evidence and the traditions of accepting testimony and physical evidence as supporting and depending on one another: testimony identifies physical evidence, while physical evidence validates testimony. The distinction between physical evidence and testimony was always clear, and each was held to be the most probative in the particular instance in which it was presented.

Evidentiary photographs and films brought into conflict assumptions about which form of evidence carried the most weight. Heliocentric and phonocentric theories came into contradiction because they were most effectively presented as a seeing; presenting them as sensuous proof required the intelligibility of testimony. Although that tension is hardly acknowledged by jurists, much of the case law concerning motion picture evidence in the 1940s and 1950s is structured by that tension.

This conflict only emerged when the use of films had become a fairly common practice. Photographs had been admitted into evidence since the 1870s. In the 1920s and 1930s, jurists reasoned that the case law governing still pictures could be applied to moving images and they too could be accepted as evidence in some cases. By 1940 the use of evidentiary films was broadly accepted in U.S. courts. Once motion pictures could in principle be shown at trials, attorneys began to offer them into evidence with increasing frequency. Protocols for their use developed through the complex negotiations between judges and lawyers and the general rules governing their use quickly split into groups of rules governing their presentation as specific types of evidence.

The Multiple Uses of Evidentiary Film

The multiple protocols for presenting evidentiary films arose from the great variety of material that can be presented through moving images, and they gave rise to divisions in the jurisprudence of evidentiary film. By the 1940s, the use of evidentiary films extended beyond the presentation of the events at issue in the case: films were also used to convey witness testimony, to illustrate the testimony of an expert witness, or to record a confession. Evidentiary films presented as *illustrations* of witness testimony, rather than *proof* of a fact, did not require elaborate testimonial. For example, with a film reenacting a crime according to a defendant's confession, it did not matter what kind of camera was used to make the film or how the film was processed because the film functions as illustrated testimony and requires only the word of the confessing defendant that the film represents the events as he experienced them.

In a 1958 note published in *American Law Reports*, left it up to the trial court to determine whether proper foundation had been laid for evidentiary films, arguing the trial court's ruling on the authentication of moving images was unlikely to be reversed by an appellate court. Such discretion allowed trial courts to deal with the wide variety of *ad hoc* situations in which motion pictures can be offered. When a general rule cannot be established covering all situations in which a certain evidentiary media might arise, case law tends to leave questions of admissibility to trial courts. Such latitude is necessary to allow the trial courts to deal with attorneys' improvised uses of motion picture evidence—uses often involving films presenting types of evidence already governed by case law—that did not explicitly address the possibility of conveying such evidence via the medium of motion pictures.

The broad discretionary authority accorded to trial courts in admitting evidentiary films stems from the pragmatic need to use a valuable means of presenting evidence, and the *ad hoc* nature of the authentication of motion picture evidence produced a variety of categories of evidentiary film, each having different effects in legal arguments. Improvisation by attorneys conditioned the courts' construal of motion pictures, presenting them as either testimony or physical evidence; for example, images could be framed as probative either because the way they were made guarantees their truth or because a witness states that they show what he saw. Though a film reenacting the testimony of a witness might be said to *prove* something, this is not because of the way the image was made but because of the witness's oath that her testimony is true. The film merely *illustrates* her testimony. Both framings of motion picture evidence became established in the juridical sphere, and each could be invoked to contest the other.

The increasing assimilation of film technology in courtrooms tended to simplify the protocol for authentication. Once films became common in the courtroom, judges came to understand the equipment and procedures needed to exhibit them as part of the infrastructure of the courts. In 1956, an appellate court in North Dakota ruled that failure to swear in the projectionist of an evidentiary film did not constitute error, over the objection of one of the litigants. The court wrote that the projectionist "merely exhibited, by mechanical means, evidence already in the record, and that the remarks of the Court directed to him were merely to ascertain if the setting and the lighting were satisfactory for the exhibition of the pictures" (Rogers) (695). This decision established a precedent whereby the projectionist was seen as part of the juridical institution whose action did not require taking an oath. Previously his projection of the film could have been construed as part of the evidence projected by the film insofar as his technique might alter the image, as the objection attempts to do. This decision established that the film itself was the evidence and the projection a mechanical convenience that allowed the evidence to reach the court. The passage of the projection of films into the infrastructure of the courts reflected a growing confidence in evidentiary film and increased familiarity with its technology.

The structure of the adversarial system itself also encouraged the constant reframing of evidentiary films between testimony and physical evidence. Some authentication procedures included aspects supporting the theory that evidentiary film was testimony, while others supported the theory that it was physical evidence. When an image is presented as physical evidence, the authenticating witness gives the time, place, and subject of the film and affirms its accuracy. If the film were only a scientific test, the images would not require confirmation that they were a fair and accurate representation of what a witness saw. The pragmatic elements of trials produce two simultaneous values for film as a medium. In arguments, lawyers can both object that a film is mere testimony and uphold a film as physical proof. This potential keeps the status of motion picture evidence floating between the two framings.

McGoorty v. Benhart: Evidentiary Film and Its Testimonial Supplement

Initially, courts required that moving images offered as physical proof of what they showed be supported by extensive testimony. Offering a film into evidence as incontrovertible proof of what it showed required the party offering the film to lay an elaborate foundation for it. Such a foundation consisted of testimony identifying the subject of the film, telling when it was made, describing the conditions under which it was made, and generally vouching for its accuracy. Quasi-paradoxically, a form of evidence offered as more convincing than an oral account had to be accounted for by oral testimony often far more extensive than a simple report of the events depicted in the film.

The use of testimony to make a film appear as an index in court can be seen in *McGoorty v. Benhart*, a 1940 personal injury case reviewed by the Appellate Court of Illinois. McGoorty brought suit against Benhart for injuries incurred in an automobile accident. The defendant claimed that the plaintiff was exaggerating his injuries. In order to prove this, Benhart entered into evidence movies of McGoorty performing certain activities that he had claimed were prevented by his injury. Benhart called to the stand the man who had made the film, Frederick A. Hurst, to authenticate the films, soliciting from him testimony to the effect that every phase of the filmmaking process had adhered to standard procedures for the production of an accurate image.

To establish that he was competent in the use of the motion picture camera, Hurst testified that for fifteen years he had been a commercial cameraman who shot films for use in courts and other places and that his most recent employer was the Stein Detective Agency. He further testified that he had taken motion pictures of McGoorty on four days in 1939 with a Bell and Howell camera in "first class working order" (*McGrooty v. Benhart*) (292), thereby guaranteeing that the film was taken with normally functioning equipment and at a time when McGoorty was supposedly injured. In testifying that the film offered was of McGoorty, Hurst identified the subject of the film. Witness testimony was the only available means by which the court could determine who the film showed, as well as when and where it was taken. Nothing in the film itself could establish these facts, which are crucial if the film was to prove anything. In order for the film to function as an index of McGoorty's physical capacity, the most basic referential, sensible functions of the film image were verified by speech.

Hurst went on to tell the court that he used three rolls of good quality film in his camera and that he could see the objects that he was photographing the whole time his camera was rolling. With that testimony, Hurst showed that there was no trickery or imperfection in the stock. It is important to note that Hurst told the court that he operated the camera in such a way as to be able to see the event he was recording while it was happening. This provided the grounds on which Hurst could verify the image itself. He went on to say that after he had taken the film he sent it to be processed by Eastman Kodak and that when he showed the film in court the image on the screen correctly portrayed what he saw at the time he made the film. Hurst thereby established that a professional laboratory had processed the film and that the movie was a true record, since the image produced faithfully depicted what he saw through the viewfinder.

Hurst's testimony established that every part of the process of producing the film was free of deception and distortion. He told the Court that he was a well-established professional and therefore a credible witness presenting a credible film. Hurst also testified that he saw the events depicted and that the film was in fact a fair and accurate representation of them. Hurst went into great detail, testifying about the exact procedure he used to make the film, describing his camera movements, when he turned the camera on and off, the speed at which the film was shot, and that film rolls had not been cut since they were removed from the camera.

In addition to Hurst's authentication, Benhart called Michael D. Francis of the Eastman Kodak Company to testify that the film had been processed "in the usual and customary manner used in the development of moving camera films" (*McGrooty v. Benhart*) (293). Francis testified that he put the reels in the processing machine himself and that they were returned to Hurst when they were finished. Both Hurst and Francis testified to their possession of the film throughout its handling. This establishes a chain of custody so that the film's whereabouts could be accounted for from the time it was shot through the time it was used in the trial. The chain of custody is meant to assure the judge and jury that the film could not have been tampered with by a third party at any point during that time. The testimony established the physical integrity of the film from the time it left the camera to its showing in court, as well as the technical norms observed in processing it.

Although the film is offered into evidence by Benhart to make the truth of what it shows self-evident to the jury, that self-evidence can only be produced by means of lengthy testimony as to every detail of the filmmaking process. The films of McGoorty's movements were meant to replace testimony as to his movements on the day on which they were shot, but they can only do so on condition of the elaboration of considerable testimony as to their own production.

Sight without Subjectivity

Evidentiary films authenticated as a form of physical evidence, such as the motion pictures in *McGoorty v. Benhart*, function in court as a form of vision, but as a vision that breaks the link between seeing and a subject and thus can be shared by multiple subjects. The human eye looks at the world with vision that terminates within a particular consciousness. For any particular person, seeing with their own eyes is seeing with their subjectivity. If the heliocentric theory of truth holds that "seeing is believing," this is because it posits a seemingly direct link between what we see and our consciousness. Unlike testimony, open to the charge of subjectivity, what we see for ourselves comes to us not from another subject but from the world—the film in *McGoorty v. Benhart* was presented as if to transform those who saw it into witnesses of what it shows. These new witnesses see for themselves. The testimony about the films production and processing conceive of it as something in the world that *shows* the world. It functioned as a supplement to vision, giving access to sights from another place and time.

In order to become a supplement to sight, an additional means of seeing that allows the courts to look at events removed in time and space,

the film in *McGoorty v. Benhart* required the extensive testimony about
its production and circulation. A film can err or become deceptive in its
chronological and geographic displacements. Anything might have
happened to the image in between the time and place the film was shot
and the time and place where it is exhibited. Nothing that can be seen in
a film vouches for what happened to its showing between the moment it
was shot and the moment it was seen. The very source of the film's
evidentiary usefulness is the source of its problematic status. In Peircian
terms, this form of evidentiary film functions as an index that has a
"dynamical" relation to what is represents but whose relation to the
senses and memory of those for whom it is a sign must be established.

The elaborate protocol for authenticating evidentiary films exemplified in *McGoorty v. Benhart* addressed the very concerns that had, in
the 1920s, made judges reluctant to admit film as evidence at all. A note
in *American Law Reports* in 1958 (considered below) cited the case as an
example of the surest protocol for getting evidentiary films admitted into
evidence. Through the late 1930s, jurists expressed concern that films
could easily be used to deceive, that the camera could be placed at a
deceptive angle or run at an abnormally high or low speed. They saw the
variety of technical procedures required to produce films as so many
opportunities for trickery: the laboratory that developed and printed the
film might distort the image; an edited film might change the events that
it rendered. Each of these suspicions is concerned with the possibility
that the film might be altered in a way that could not be detected and
that such an alteration would harness the persuasive force of seeing to
something false. Though many of these suspicions might also be held
about photographs, film was even more suspect of the persuasive supplement accorded to film and its depiction of movement. When evidentiary motion pictures gained widespread acceptance in the early
1940s, each of these concerns called for the testimony of a witness to the
process by which the film was made. Not only did the use of evidentiary
films require an exhaustive testimonial foundation, it also required that
the production of the image be overseen. The rhetorical power of evidentiary film depends on the knowledge that the image was not distorted
in the interval between the time and place of what it shows and its
exhibition in court.

The extensive testimonial foundation laid for the films used in
McGoorty v. Benhart assured the jury of the integrity of the films across

that interval. Every step in the production of the films was guaranteed to be free of distortion, and every moment was accounted for in the films' journey from the riverside where they were recorded to the courtroom.

Evidentiary film is a repeatable sight that, as it were, stops short of the seeing subject. An evidentiary film does not invite the viewer to ask who is looking. The film's spectator sees the film from his own point of view, as if the film's vision terminated in his own consciousness without another in between. Evidentiary films were framed as a seeing that could circulate between subjects without being a subjective point of view. Since the rhetorical force of evidentiary films was based on their objectivity, the scopic field of particular subjects had to be excluded from evidentiary films. For a film to render the point of view of a subject meant that the film was itself subjective. Evidentiary film provided a vision that was objective for each subject that sees it.

Hurst's testimony in *McGoorty v. Benhart* can be understood as defensive, anticipating and foreclosing attacks that the plaintiff might make on the films. The courts were afraid that editing could radically alter what appeared on screen and therefore deceive jurors. According to a particular cinematic definition of editing, Hurst did in fact edit his film. He used what is called "in-camera editing" to allow him to follow McGoorty performing actions in different areas. Hurst would turn off the camera when McGoorty changed locations, set up again in the new space and turn the camera back on. The court was not suspicious of this technique because each activity performed by McGoorty is shown in one continuous shot. Each activity shown can be seen as a unit of evidence; each shot is equivalent to the statement that McGoorty did something demonstrating that his injuries were not as extensive as he claimed. Furthermore, Hurst's testimony accounted for every instance of in-camera editing and justified every cut it in terms of McGoorty's movements. Thus Hurst's testimony about the beginning and end of each shot assured the court that the films were not meant to trick the viewer. Hurst's in-camera editing preserved the physical continuity of each reel of film. That proved that the film did not undergo an additional editing process after it was printed and thus seemed to be an further indication that the film had not been tampered with.

The testimony authenticating the film in *McGoorty v. Benhart* implies that the film functions as a scientific test, an index of what it shows. By insisting on the fact that normal photographic procedures were used to make and process the film, the witnesses were in effect arguing that those procedures always produce a veridical image. The film both superseded and was supported by oral testimony, bringing the heliocentric and phonocentric theories of evidence into tension. It required the rampant multiplication of the testimony to make the film appear as more reliable than any testimony.

This multiplication of testimony did not escape the attention of opposing counsel. On appeal, McGoorty cited the admission of the films as judicial error on the basis that there was a witness present in court who had been present at the scene and who could testify as to what he saw there—namely the cameraman Hurst. The appellant argued that this made the film merely cumulative and that it was not the best evidence of what happened. Such an attribution of error treats the films as a lower form of evidence than testimony and assumes that the court would favor oral testimony where it was possible to have it. The appeals court found for Benhart, citing the testimonial procedure used to authenticate the film as exemplary.

Standardization, Simplification, Slippage

The protocol used in *McGoorty v. Benhart* became the model form of authentication recommended by authoritative legal texts. The 1958 *American Law Reports* note on motion picture evidence suggests a four-part protocol for authentication of films (Rogers) (692–695). The first part consists of giving evidence about the circumstances under which the film was made, the qualifications of the camera operator, the type of camera lenses and films used, and so on. The second part consists of evidence about the circumstances surrounding the processing of the film. The third part consists of evidence about the projector, its speed and distance from the screen. The fourth part is testimony by someone present at the scene when the pictures were taken who can testify as to their accuracy. Like the procedure used by Benhart, this protocol seeks to establish motion picture evidence as more reliable than witness testimony by establishing that the films being offered have been made and exhibited in such a way as to make the spectator a witness to the event. It is only because the image is expected to function as physical proof that testimony about the procedure used to produce it is necessary. If the films were offered as an illustrated form of testimony, testimony that the film produced a fair and accurate representation of the filmed event would be sufficient proof of the picture's authenticity.

An evidentiary film gives jurors the impression of being the act of looking at what it depicts and the sense of having seen something directly, which increases the persuasive power of the film. This effect becomes a rhetorical supplement that is the source of the evidentiary film's persuasive power. Evidentiary films give the jury the impression of seeing the event for themselves and thus engage the rhetoric that "seeing is believing." This rhetorical aspect of evidentiary films can also be understood as a supplement of seemingly unedited seeing, of seeing-for-oneself, that inheres in the motion picture image.

By the late 1950s, more cases appeared in which films were authenticated merely by the testimony of a witness at the scene when the films were shot.[1] The witness stated that the film fairly and accurately depicted the events shown; this was sufficient foundation to render a film admissible as evidence. This shift seems like a natural trend toward simplification motivated by the court's growing familiarity with, and confidence in, motion picture technology. It is much more efficient to authenticate a film with the short testimony of one witness than to spend court time laying a foundation for every aspect of filmmaking. However, this streamlining implied a fundamental change in the assumptions that the courts were making about films. While the more elaborate foundation required to authenticate motion pictures emphasized the indexical possibilities of the medium—treating films as physical evidence or scientific tests—the new, simpler, foundation treated them as witness testimony. The elaborate protocol for authentication both establishes and emphasizes the scientific validity of the filmed image. Under the new method of identification, films were framed by the court as a particularly effective means of presenting what a witness saw.

Malingering and the Rhetorical Force of Evidentiary Films

Cases centering on the issue of malingering were of particular importance for the development of case law governing the use of motion picture evidence. Such cases make palpable the effects of presenting evidentiary film as either physical proof or illustrated testimony. They bring up key issues in the use of motion picture evidence, such as the use of film to prove a fact, the temporal framing of an event, and the interpretation of what is seen in the image.

In malingering cases, films were presented in support of three principal points in arguments: to illustrate an expert's theory about the causes and consequences of an accident; to show the court the location where the accident took place; and to provide evidence that the plaintiff had exaggerated his injuries. When insurance companies and other defendants felt that a claimant was not as disabled as she claimed, the defendant would arrange to have the claimant filmed while engaged in activities that she claimed she could not perform. Malingering films, a prominent genre of motion picture evidence starting in the late 1920s and continuing through the present day, increased in use dramatically between 1940 and 1958,[2] when such films became an established practice for insurance companies and others involved in personal injury litigation. Films showing the claimant performing actions incompatible with his claimed disability were effective in convincing juries that the claimants were malingering. The frequency with which the court's admission of such films was cited as error by appellants shows that the jurisprudence surrounding their use was still catching up to the practice itself.

The use of malingering films brought important issues of policy as well as issues of law, to the attention of the courts. Judges expressed concern about the implications of filming plaintiffs without their knowledge or consent, a concern heightened in cases in which the claimant had been lured into the situation filmed by operatives of the insurance company. *Maryland Casualty Company v. Coker* (1941) exemplifies such cases. James Coker, who was injured at work, claimed total and permanent injury. Before the trial began in federal court in Texas, an agent of Maryland Casualty named Banks invited Coker on a fishing trip "with female companions and the usual liquid refreshments" and a hidden cameraman shot film of this expedition (*Maryland Casualty Company v. Coker*) (44). At trial, the motion pictures were presented purporting to show Coker rowing the boat used for the trip, something his injuries should not have allowed. Coker claimed that he did not know that Banks was in the employ of the insurance company.

The trial judge in *Maryland Casualty Company v. Coker* was deeply troubled by the way in which the film of the fishing trip was made. He expressed distaste for the trap laid by the insurance company, but saw no legal principle that allowed him to exclude the film from the trial. The judge stated, "As to policy I don't approve of the methods employed, but I assume under the general rules of law that the jury is entitled to see the pictures and the jury can take into consideration the method employed to secure them and have the pictures made" (*Maryland Casualty Company v. Coker*) (44). The propriety of the films was a matter of legislative policy rather than a matter of legal principle. In overruling an objection to the motion pictures, the trial judge said that he recognized "the merit of the objection to the effect that it is violating the sense of fairness, propriety and good morals to take pictures in the way these pictures were taken" (44). The defendant's appeal, based on the trial judge's comments, claimed reversible error. The trial judge's statements show a strong social concern yet to be addressed by the law. The defendant felt that the judge's commentary influenced the jury to find for the plaintiff.

In his opinion for the Fifth Circuit Court of Appeals, Judge Foster wrote that while "it would have been better if the remarks of the Court had remained unsaid" (44), they did not constitute reversible error. Foster felt compelled to enter into the discussion concerning the propriety of the manner in which the films were taken, although in itself this was not one of the issues in the appeal. That he did so is a further indication of the weight of concerns raised by such films. While Foster recognized that motion pictures taken to show malingering must perforce be taken surreptitiously, he argued that "when the defendant induces the plaintiff to put himself into a position where such pictures may be taken, the situation is somewhat analogous to entrapment in a criminal case" (44).

This concern is also apparent in the opinion of Judge Rufus L. Thompson of the Third Appellate District Court of California in the 1940 case of *A. L. Harmon v. San Joaquin Light & Power Corporation*. Thompson was wary of the "modern art of photography and the devices of an ingenious director" (*Harmon v. San Joaquin Light & Power Corporation*) (174). He cited as authorities on this subject both a note in the 1933 volume of *American Law Reports* (1315) and a 1940 *Reader's Digest* article entitled "Tricked into Acting" (71–73) about the Hollywood technique of shooting a rehearsal without telling their actors that the cameras are rolling. *Reader's Digest* seems an odd authority in a legal opinion, but since the situation concerned filming subjects without their knowledge (save that those subjects are not litigants but actors), the judge used the citation as *doxa* to point to his uneasiness about this practice. Prior to this citation, Thompson noted that though the plaintiff criticized the secretive way the films were taken, that issue need not be discussed in the opinion. It would seem that such a discussion was very much on the judge's mind, even though he could not find the legal grounds for indulging in it.

Temporal Selection and the Out-of-Frame

Motion picture evidence is always framed by its spatial and temporal limits. That which lies beyond the edges of the frame or happened before or after the camera rolled can always be invoked in an argument that a film excludes something which would radically change the appearance of its image. Films offered as evidence that a plaintiff is not as disabled as she claims to be can only represent the plaintiff at certain moments; they cannot show the claimant for the entire period after the injury was incurred. Only a portion of the claimant's activity can be presented to the court in motion pictures, because the court does not have the time to view films of the claimant's entire life since the disability was acquired and because it would be impractical to make such films. As a result of this temporal framing, the claimant can always argue that the moments rendered in the film are not representative of the state of her health over a long period of time. Thus, the problem of temporal selection was imposed on malingering films.

This presented the courts with the legal problem of whether the actions performed by the plaintiff during the time when the film was shot constitute proof that the plaintiff was not disabled. Jurists had to decide whether claims of disability could be disproved by the accomplishment of a small number of physical acts whose performance the putative disability would impede. This issue caused the courts major consternation and, in some cases, the same films were read in different ways by different courts.

In the case of *DeBattiste v. Laudadio*, three different judicial bodies produced conflicting interpretations of the same films. In 1945, DeBattiste, a construction worker, was thrown from his employer's truck by a collision. DeBattiste filed a claim with the Workman's Compensation Board for partial disability. He received total disability benefits for the work time he missed as a result of injury. When he returned to work, his compensatory payments were suspended because his regular pay remained the same as it had been, leading the board to conclude that his disability had not caused a loss of earning capacity. Three months later, DeBattiste filed to have his benefits restored because his wages had since been cut from one dollar an hour to fifty cents an hour. After a series of appeals by both DeBattiste and his employer's insurance company, the case was brought before the Court of Common Pleas of Philadelphia County. At that trial, the insurance company offered as evidence motion pictures of DeBattiste at work, taken after his accident. The court admitted these films over the plaintiff's objections. While the Court of Common Pleas was considering the case, the insurance company petitioned the Workman's Compensation Board for a new hearing to review the motion pictures. The board granted the petition.

The board found that the four hundred feet of film presented by the defendant did not conclusively show that DeBattiste was not disabled. These motion pictures showed the defendant doing heavy work on four days over the period of a month in the spring of 1947. Their episodic character weighed heavily in the board's decision. They concluded that the films "disclose claimant's activity for a period of twenty minutes and took sixteen minutes to show. The five reels were fastened together and do not show claimant's continuous activity for any extended period of time" (*DeBattiste v. Anthony Laudadio & Son et al.*, 1950) (40). The board was concerned about the selective nature of the films presented by the insurance company. The films only showed DeBattiste hard at work in a series of short shots. Accordingly, they did not convince the board of DeBattiste's capacity for sustained effort, a capacity he would have needed to continue as a construction worker. The board was concerned with what happened in segments of time before and after each individual shot, which were omitted from the series of discontinuous shots presented.

Unlike the Workman's Compensation Board, which argued that the films left out too much to prove that DeBattiste was not disabled, the Court of Common Pleas was only concerned with what the films did show. In reviewing the decision of the board, the court wrote,

> We do not think that the pictures can be so lightly brushed aside. They furnish absolutely incontrovertible proof that the claimant can lift his

injured arm above his head and otherwise use it in ways that he claimed
he could not. . . . In fact, they support but one conclusion and that is
that the claimant suffers no impairment of the ability to do the heavy
work of a laborer (*DeBattiste v. Anthony Laudadio & Son, et al.*) (42).

The Court of Common Pleas interpreted the law governing disability
claims so that evidence that *at any time after the injury* the claimant
performed actions his disability putatively prevented him from doing
invalidated his claim. The Court of Common Pleas reasoned that—since
the films were properly authenticated by the cameraman who had swon
that they were taken on certain days in 1947—and since DeBattiste had
been identified as the subject in the films, they constituted irrefutable
indices of the actions of the claimant, actions that proved that he was not
disabled.

The Court of Common Pleas' decision shows the force of evidentiary film presented as physical evidence. In construing the film presented as an index of the actions of its subject, the Court of Common
Pleas gave it precedence over any contradictory testimony in the case.
The court wrote in its decision that because the films "support only one
conclusion . . . the oral testimony and medical opinion to the contrary
must be disregarded" (*DeBattiste v. Anthony Laudadio & Son et al.*) (42).

When DeBattiste appealed to the Superior Court of Pennsylvania,
Judge Chester H. Rhodes insisted on seeing the film, although it was
not formally entered into evidence. In his 1950 opinion, Rhodes wrote
that while the films were admissible, they were not conclusive in this
particular case. He questioned the legal theory that the case could be
settled by incontrovertible physical facts, noting that "the question of the
extent of physical disability and consequent loss of earning power is a
complex factual matter dependent on many variables" (43). He asked how
DeBattiste's earning ability before the accident compared with his earning
ability after the accident and whether the pictures showed him working
more or less quickly than before the accident. Rhodes ruled that the
testimony of two physicians, DeBattiste's employer, and an impartial expert
appointed by the board were better sources of information about DeBattiste's disability than the films. Whether the isolated scenes of the films
proved disability or not was debated by three judicial bodies, indicating the
difficulty and importance of the temporal limits of an evidentiary film, as
well as something more radical.

Rhodes's argument against the probative value of the films is significantly different than the board's argument. Where the board only

criticized the temporal selectivity of the films, Rhodes argued also that as a matter of legal principle a disability case such as this one cannot be decided on the basis of anything visible in a film of the kind presented by the insurance carrier. Rhodes found that proof of disability and loss of wages resulting from it required a comparison of the claimant's ability to work and make money before and after the injury. According to the judge, such a comparison might be better made in testimony than in motion pictures. If such a comparison could be articulated in a film at all, it would require a much more complex form than that of the film presented in this case. Besides the fact that such a film would almost certainly require footage of the claimant at work before the injury—when the insurer had no reason to film him—such a complex film would have been self-defeating in this period. The rhetorical sophistication of such a film would have aroused suspicion of manipulation.

Each of the three interpretations of the films emphasizes a different interpretation of the motion picture medium by the law. The Workman's Compensation Board based its evaluation on the discrepancy between the short, discontinuous duration of the films and the longer, continuous duration of DeBattiste's life. The Court of Common Pleas discounted the testimony of experts because it viewed the films as incontrovertible evidence of physical facts. Lastly, the superior court saw the films as inconclusive because the issues at stake in the case were not directly visible but needed to be proven through comparison. All three of these distinct interpretations assume that films are a form of physical evidence. The board and the superior court ruled that the testimony of the medical experts was more probative than the films only because the motion pictures did not show anything that proved that DeBattiste was not injured. If they had, presumably, they would have been given more weight than the oral testimony. Yet, in the superior court decision, the question of the indexicality of the film was less important than the question of whether or not the case at hand can be proved by anything that could be directly seen.

Perception and the Out-of-Frame

When the defense in the DeBattiste case attempted to use films to suggest to the jury that the plaintiff was not at all disabled, they attempted to use the films to convince the jury of something invisible. An even more egregious attempt to use film to show something that could not be seen appears in the case of *A. L. Harmon v. San Joaquin Light and Power Corporation.* On June 2, 1937, Harmon was on horseback driving a herd of cattle. He inadvertently touched a cut power cable and twelve thousand volts of electricity passed through his body, killing his horse, six head of cattle, and seriously injuring Harmon. Harmon claimed that, among other disabilities, his vision was affected and that he became deaf as a result of the accident. The defense entered into evidence films of Harmon throwing a ball with a "young lady" (*A. L. Harmon v. San Joauquin Light & Power Corporation*) (174) as conclusive proof that his disabilities were less than he claimed.

The films entered into evidence in *Harmon* were silent and thus could not show the plaintiff failing to respond to a sound. Even if the defense had produced films that implied Harmon's deafness, they would not have constituted incontrovertible proof of his deafness. Framed as physical evidence, motion pictures can only prove something if they can be a direct index of it. A film could only show a behavior from which deafness could be inferred, not the deafness itself. A soundtrack of a gun going off in close proximity to a human figure who does not react to the report at all might imply deafness, but it does not show deafness directly.

In his 1940 opinion, Judge Thompson of the Third Appellate District Court of California noted that the films "throw no light on the plaintiff's alleged deafness" (174). Reading the judge's phrase literally exposes the problem of the representation of invisible phenomena in evidentiary films. No evidentiary film can show deafness directly, because deafness is not visible. Deafness is invisible insofar as it is the absence of auditory perception. Not only is the auditory itself invisible, perceptions cannot be directly represented by evidentiary film since this would render the film subjective. To show what someone heard, a film must present a subjectively *perceived* world rather than an objectively *perceivable* world. Perforce, a film showing a perception must be a seeing that solicits a seeing subject between the scene it shows and the audience. Since an evidentiary film's persuasive power is weakened by the imposition of a subject between the perceived scene and the jury, evidentiary film can only imply a failure of perception by showing a person failing to respond to a sensible stimulus.

The same limitations apply to the defense's use of the films to show Harmon's ability to see. A restricted field of vision could not be represented by an evidentiary film both directly and objectively at the same time. The film of Harmon playing catch was presented to imply that his field of vision was in no way impaired. However, this is not the only inference that could be drawn from the film. In his opinion, Judge Thompson makes much of the difference between what a film shows directly and what it implies. He explicitly states that films and photographs "which absolutely refute the conclusion to be drawn from oral testimony regarding a particular fact should be conclusive on that particular subject" (173). He constructs motion pictures as a reliable index.

Judge Thompson points out that it is possible that the person throwing Harmon the ball "took particular pains to toss the ball within the narrow radius of his vision" (174). He notes that the film does not make it clear how far away Harmon's partner was standing or the speed at which she was throwing the ball. Establishing those facts might have strengthened the implication that Harmon's vision was unimpaired. But the particular motion pictures offered by the defense were not conclusive on the issue of Harmon's disability. They attempted to show something that could not be seen. Like the films showing selective actions performed by the plaintiff in the DeBattiste case, the films of Harmon *implied* something rather than functioned as an index of what they meant to prove. This use of evidentiary film seeks to shine the persuasive light of the heliocentric theory of truth onto a fact that is not shown directly and in so doing increases the risk of challenges invoking the out-of-frame.

The judge argued that the film's off-screen space was indeterminate and that this ambiguity cast serious doubt on the charge of malingering. Invoking activity beyond the spatial or temporal frame of evidentiary film tends to weaken its persuasive force by suggesting another explanation for what it shows and by pointing to the subjective character of spatial and temporal selection. What the film does not show is used to change or cast into doubt the meaning of what can be seen in the image. This technique is in a sense a reframing of the film. The film in *Harmon* was presented as if the edges of the image presented a limit to inquiry. In his opinion, the judge enlarged that frame and in so doing turned the image into an ambiguous, more subjective one. As in this case, the out-of-frame is usually invoked to render an image indeterminate: asking what lies beyond the frame casts into doubt the original implication. It is not necessary to draw another inference from the image in order to invalidate the one that we have already been asked to draw. The out-of-frame brings the force of negation to bear on an image—a power that appears by virtue of the juridical interpretation of film as a medium.

The out-of-frame was less problematic for films that were not construed as physical evidence. In *Maryland Casualty Company v. Coker*, the appellate court found that "in the last analysis motion pictures displayed to the jury are entitled to no more weight than the testimony of a reliable witness" (44). This is a reasonable conclusion given that all moving images entered into evidence are authenticated by witness testimony. Only testimony can authenticate the film as a fair and accurate representation. For example, in the 1956 case of *International Union, United Automobile, Aircraft and Agricultural Implement Workers of America, C. I. O. et al. v. Paul S. Russell*, the judge explicitly stated that evidentiary films were to be regarded as "pictorial communication of witness testimony" (*International Union*) (470). Nevertheless the appeal of evidentiary films for litigants is that they can be more persuasive than oral testimony because such films connote indexicality even when the foundation laid for them establishes them as testimony.

Motion pictures in court were thus caught in a variable framing, sometimes appearing as testimony and sometimes appearing as physical evidence. The effects of these two frames extended beyond the court's interpretation of the indexicality of film as medium. They effected what could be argued about moving images: if courts framed motion pictures as testimony, further testimony could be solicited to clarify what the films showed; if they framed films as physical evidence, then unless what they showed was beyond the understanding of the "reasonable man," the interpretation of any particular film entered into evidence was up to the jury. The nonsubjectivity of evidentiary films affords the juror his own objective view of what the film depicts. In the 1952 case *Mary B. Williamson v. St. Louis Public Service Company*, the plaintiff testified that a film of her walking, entered into evidence by the Public Service Company, did not show her normal gait. On appeal the defense cited Williamson's testimony as reversible error. The Public Service Company argued that "the pictures spoke for themselves" and that "anyone could see what they showed" (*Mary B. Williamson v. St. Louis Public Service Company*). The assignment of error shows that when framed as physical proof the interpretation of an evidentiary film was to be done directly by the jury.[3]

Conclusion

In the 1940s and 1950s films were presented as either an illustrated form of witness testimony or as physical proof of what they showed. Films were offered as evidence both of directly visible matters and of facts that could only be inferred from what could be seen. Thus, evidentiary films varied in their value as proof. Although films were introduced into the courts as a more reliable form of evidence than testimony, they had to be identified and guaranteed by a witness. The requirement of a testimonial foundation for evidentiary films not only meant that the credibility of a given film varied according to how that foundation was laid, it also produced a crisis in the philosophical premises upon which evidentiary law founds itself. It did so by bringing two theories of truth, one based on seeing evidence and the other on hearing testimony, into conflict. Within this crisis, evidentiary films held the problematic position of an objective form of vision. The objectivity of evidentiary film was always threatened by its repeatability, since the iteration of a film leaves behind the context in which it was taken. Once a film is shown in a new context, its objectivity can be challenged by invoking what lays outside its frame. The courts imposed various strictures on evidentiary films to ensure both their objectivity and their repeatability.

The development of case law to govern the use of film first reversed and then disarticulated traditional evidentiary hierarchies; a unified concept of evidentiary film gave way to a growing multiplicity of categories. As we have seen, much of this case law addressed the conditions in which a film could be admitted as evidence and what a film could be used to prove. When evidentiary films were offered as physical proof of what they show, every aspect of their production had to be guaranteed by witness testimony. When the authentication of evidentiary film is reduced to testimony that the film is a fair and accurate representation of what a witness saw, the film becomes "pictorial communication of witness testimony" (*International Union*).

Traditionally, testimony had been considered to be the most reliable form of evidence. In many cases films were offered as conclusive proof of what they showed and presented as a way to discredit testimony. The use of heliocentric evidence overturned the phonocentric hierarchy of evidence in general. Yet when a film was presented as physical evidence of what it showed, it had to be authenticated by extensive testimony guaranteeing every aspect of its production. This requirement meant that although film could appear as more probative than testimony it did not inaugurate a stable heliocentric hierarchy of evidence. The heliocentric truth of film had to be carried by a testimonial host.

The deconstruction inaugurated by the projection of film in the courtroom renders possible the effects of contamination and perversity outlined in this chapter. Although not all forms of evidentiary film are framed as physical evidence, the indexical potential of film comes to be a connotation of the medium in general. This means that films can be offered in attempts to convince the jury of what is not true and even of what is not visible. In response to these problems, the courts improvised a constant vigilance.

The cases analyzed in this chapter illustrate the process by which film's value as an evidentiary medium was produced by the pragmatic conditions of trial procedure. As in many interpretations of cinematic moving images, film comes to connote indexicality, but the form and purpose of that indexicality is not the same as in the cinema. In the cinema such indexicality, when it appears, is an implicit result of the medium itself and works to give the spectator an impression of reality. In court, film's indexicality is a result of the combination of a particular image and the testimony authenticating it and functions to purvey the truth of an event to the jury. Unlike cinematic images, evidentiary films are foreclosed from depicting subjectivity. The next chapter will show that as courts became even more familiar with motion pictures they tended to take their indexicality more and more for granted.

4

Framing Videotape

In the late 1960s the introduction in the United States of the first
portable video recording system, the Sony Portapak, increased the
legal community's interest in the use of motion picture evidence. The
introduction of video evidence into trial procedures and of video
equipment into courthouse infrastructure completely integrated moving
images into U.S. legal culture and linked courts to the circulation of
electronic images through society at large. Video served the purpose of
the courts better than film, and was readily integrated into courthouses
and trial procedures. Showing a tape disrupts trial procedure less than
projecting a film does (e.g., the courtroom lights need not be dimmed),
video is easier to authenticate than film, and there is no need for testimony about the reliability of the laboratory that developed it because
videos come out of the camera ready to screen. Furthermore, by the mid-
1970s, the mass manufacture of ever more portable, progressively simpler,
and less expensive videotape equipment rendered the use of moving
images in court even more attractive. Soon, video would become much
more common in court than film ever had been.

The prior use of the phrase "motion pictures" in appeals courts
rulings facilitated the legal transition from the courtroom use of film to
that of video. Since the rubric "motion pictures" could easily be interpreted to include video, the precedent for admitting tapes had already
been set. From the late 1960s on, case law has tended to use the terms
"film," "video," and "motion pictures" interchangeably. A functional

equivalence was established between film and video within juridical discourse. This taxonomic interpretation, the use of one broad category instead of two narrower ones, is an important part of the way that motion picture evidence is framed in court. Although the physical differences between video and film can be a crucial element of interpretation among film scholars, it has never been important to the courts.

The shift from film to video prompted a period in which the moving image's jurisprudence rapidly developed. The integration of the moving image into trial procedure was accompanied by a change in the court's interpretation of motion pictures—and particularly of movies as a means of showing the truth. Earlier courts saw moving images as a potentially duplicitous class of evidence capable of persuading jurors to make unfounded judgments. Judges had been concerned that films "may be made very deceptive by the operator of the machine used in taking the pictures" (*Massachusetts Bonding & Ins. Co. v. Worthy*) (393). However, between the early 1970s and the early 1990s, judges viewed the most trustworthy means for conveying evidence., a medium that could be completely authenticated.

In *Video Techniques in Trial and Pretrial*, John C. Buchanan, Carol D. Bos, and Fred I. Heller write that moving images have "the capability, if properly used, to communicate an accurate message to the jury like no other medium can" (Heller, 1983). Video accomplishes this function as well as film, but the ease with which video could be produced and exhibited meant that it was practical to use in quotidian procedures.

The courts initially used video as a means of recording depositions—a practice for which the medium offered numerous advantages. Economical and efficient, it could convey the demeanor of the witness and could be edited to keep inadmissible testimony out of court. Expert witnesses could be taped at their convenience before the start of a trial so that the presentation of complex testimony no longer depended on their availability. In addition, when considering objections made to videotaped depositions, the judge could order the offending statements to be deleted before the video was shown at trial, so that in a taped deposition, the excluded questions and answers would never be heard by the jury. (In ordinary testimony, if the judge upholds an objection, she strikes the statement from the record and instructs the jury to disregard it—but the jury could not "unhear" it.)

Starting in the 1970s, courtroom protocols increasingly allowed depositions to be recorded on videotape. In 1970, a legal change accommodated this emerging practice when the rule prescribing the forms of deposition accepted in federal civil cases—Federal Rule of Civil Procedure 30(b)(4)—was amended to allow presentation of depositions recorded by "other than stenographic means." Most state jurisdictions subsequently made similar amendments to their rules of civil procedure.

Prerecorded videotaped trials were first used in Ohio in simple civil litigation. These trials introduced cameras, monitors, and editing bays into the courts' equipment pools, and all the testimony was recorded on videotape. Both parties' attorneys were present at the recording sessions, as was a camera operator with the power to swear in the witnesses. Whereas early evidentiary film projectionists were sometimes suspected of falsifying what they screened, the video deposition cameraman had the authority to administer an oath. The attorneys, as in traditional testimony, offered objections and responses during the taking of the deposition, a judge reviewed the tapes and had inadmissible questions and testimony edited out before the tape was shown in open court. The process of jury selection, opening and closing statements, judicial instructions happened face to face. In trials in which all the testimony was prerecorded and judges ruled on objections before the case came before a jury, jurors were protected from any inadmissible information, and a significant amount of time was saved as well (McCrystal, 1978). In many civil cases where all the witness testimony was prerecorded, a trial could be averted by an out-of-court settlement, since all the testimony was known to both sides and the verdict was therefore more predictable.

U.S. courts generally assimilated videotape deliberately and efficiently, unlike film, which was adopted as the result of the various local judicial responses to films offered by attorneys. In 1974, the Federal Justice Center established a pilot video program to promote the use of videotape in courts, to evaluate its potential, and "through experience to develop rules and procedures for the future use of the medium in courts" (*Guidelines*) (ix). The pilot projects used single-camera, black-and-white recording systems. The courts in the program also received simple editing equipment to eliminate inadmissible testimony together with courtroom monitors to allow judge, jury, and counsel to see the playback. On the basis of these pilot programs, the Federal Justice Center issued the first edition of *Guidelines For Pre-Recording Testimony on Videotape Prior to Trial* in 1974. Interest in videotaped depositions ran so high that the Federal Justice Center had to issue a second printing in 1976.

The Federal Justice Center's *Guidelines for Pre-Recording Testimony on Videotape Prior to Trial*: Policy and Pragmatics

Before video could replace stenographic transcripts of depositions, courts had to ensure that tapes were at least as accurate a means of recording testimony. This process was abetted by the small but persistent amount of error associated with stenographic transcripts and by lawyers' complaints about the difficulty of holding jurors' attention with a monotonous reading from a transcript. However, since stenography had traditionally been the accepted means of presenting the testimony of a witness not present at the trial, it was the standard by which any new means would be measured.

Although courts considered the videotaping as a better means of recording testimony than stenography—because it preserved the witness's demeanor—they initially feared that videotape could give the impression of being a revelation of the truth, carrying connotations that council could take advantage of in illegitimate ways. Jurists held video in suspicion because of the rhetorical surplus associated with moving images. In the case of videotaped depositions, jurists also worried that camera angles or editing techniques might be used in deceitful ways to prejudice the jury. If videotapes were to be a means of juridical communication, one integrated into courthouses rather than merely presented by lawyers, the courts had to regulate their *form* carefully. Left unregulated, videotaped depositions might seem to jurors to be the equivalent of live testimony while subtly introducing a bias.

According to the Federal Justice Center's *Guidelines for Pre-Recording Testimony on Videotape Prior to Trial*,[1] "the objective of videotaping testimony is to simulate the personal appearance of the witness" (23). The simulation of personal appearance allows videotapes to convey the witness's demeanor, which the jury uses to assess their credibility. The demeanor of the witness depicted in the video is the source of the pragmatic justification of video's privilege over a written deposition—it meets a need to see the witness in a way that a transcript cannot.

The *Guidelines* assume demeanor is assessed primarily through visual cues. Although videotape and audiotape both preserve the inflections of the witness's speech, video is the preferred means of display because it allows the jury to see the witness. There is little mention of the importance of the witness's tones of voice in judging credibility. By downplaying the importance of the vocal texture of the testimony in judging its veracity, the courts reduce the aural component of speech to verbalization without any grain or body from which statements issue.

Compared with the many types of shots and camera styles used in commercial television and film production, the *Guidelines* prescribe a very restricted set of shots for use in the production of videotaped depositions and prerecorded videotaped trials. These restrictions were developed to meet the court's requirement of objectivity. Three types of shots predominated in videotaped depositions in this period: (1) the head-and-shoulders close-up of a witness; (2) the medium shot of the witness's waist to just above her head; and (3) the long shot from head to foot. All these shots are taken from about the same height as the subject (Miller, 1979) (153).

Along with recommending these particular shots, the *Guidelines* offer warnings and suggestions regarding each type of shot. Long shots may hide the physical traits of a witness, for example, whereas close-ups tend to exaggerate them. Close-ups are particularly suited for small evidentiary objects (*Guidelines*) (23–24). The *Guidelines* recommend the use of these shots because they allow the jury to see that "the witness's appearance is not distorted by impermissibly suggestive camera techniques" (23). Such shots are also recommended because they are objective and do not distract the jury. The recommended shots exclude the possibility of a point-of-view shot in order to prevent the proceedings from appearing subjective, just as other kinds of evidentiary motion pictures avoid point-of-view shots and their subjectivity.

The *Guidelines* claim to present an objective form for videotaping testimony without the support of experimental data. Common sense suggests that the recommended shots are objective because commercial television and cinema use them to convey objective facts (rather than shots from an extremely high angle, shots that suggest the point of view of someone in an unusual position, or shots that aggrandize their subjects).

However, it is far from clear whether these shots are objective or whether they signify objectivity in the cinema. In certain instances they do both; in other cases they connote objectivity without having an objective relation to their referents.

Certain witnesses appear more credible when seen on tape; the shots prescribed by the court indicate that the presentation is objective, but the rhetorical effect of the medium, its surplus persuasive value, makes the witness more believable (Miller and Fontes, 73). If such a mode of presentation is used to make testimony appear more credible, then it is not objective.

The semiotics of videotaped depositions includes syntactic rules about the sequences of shots as well as semantic rules about the kinds of shots that can be used. The *Guidelines* prescribe protocols for the elimination and reordering of shots, for turning the camera off, for camera movements, and for the order in which the recommended shot scales should be used. In addition to their stated purpose—"to make the videotape an objective and factual, but nonetheless interesting, document" (23)—these rules work to make the tapes as easy as possible for the jury to follow.

According to the *Guidelines*, depositions should start with a long or establishing shot, showing all the participants. During testimony the operator should pan and zoom to a medium shot of the witness and occasionally move in for a close-up of the witness's whole face (23–24). The *Guidelines* justify reframing the shot because "our typical experience with [video] involves frequent changes in the picture presented to us" (x). To keep the viewers' attention, the operator should move the camera at least every four to five minutes. The *Guidelines* here use ordinary commercial production practices and viewing habits to determine the form best suited to courtroom use. Such a derivation shows that the Federal Justice Center reasoned from *doxa* about video and television, like the jurists who initially framed evidentiary film on the basis of what they knew about movies.

In general, the *Guidelines* try to provide a form of video that will give as much information as possible about all the participants in a deposition. But the competing desire to keep the jurors' attention supersedes the goal of giving a complete simulation of the proceedings. The *Guidelines* assume that the "media 'principles'" (x) that govern continuity in commercial film and television apply to videotaped depositions.

The *Guidelines* anchor these principles in the material character of video as signifier. They point to the low resolution of the long shot as a factor that decreases the viewer's attention span and asserts that video is a "close-up medium" (23). This is an argument about the kinds of signs that video is best suited to present, in which the rules are justified by reference to characteristics of the medium.

The *Guidelines* rely on television and film production standards in an attempt to ensure that its standards convey witnesses' testimony as clearly as possible. They assume that the more familiar the structure of a tape is to jurors, the easier it will be to follow. For example, the *Guidelines* state that all participants in the deposition should be kept in the same spatial relationship established in the opening shot (26). If the participants move around the room while the camera is not on them, the operator should pull back to a new establishing shot (27). The sudden appearance of a participant in an unanticipated position not only runs the risk of being confusing, but it also might constitute an unintended message about the matter being deposed. For the same reasons, the *Guidelines* say that all camera movements should be "smooth and even," not "disturbing" (27). By eliminating jump cuts, swish pans, and other unfamiliar syntax, the *Guidelines* guard against the introduction of bias.

The *Guidelines* prescribe rules that are specific to videotaped depositions. It requires the video operator to announce on the tape that the session is going off-record when the camera is stopped to change positions or reload tape (26). This rule is a significant departure from the norms of commercial production, the conventions of which usually attempt to efface the mechanics of the camera. The announcement that the session is going off-record allays any suspicion of improper editing when the tape is shown in court and conforms to the procedure required in written transcripts to explicitly mark points when members of the court say something off the record. Since jump cuts are ruled out, any sudden change in the image that is not announced would be readily apparent and could be questioned by council. By providing a form that attempts to ensure a tape's objectivity, the policies set out in the *Guidelines* try to prevent judges from excluding videotaped depositions on principle. In so doing, the *Guidelines* rely on arguments both about how motion pictures signify in general and how they should signify in court.

The Federal Justice Center policies were so successful, and the use of videotaped depositions so popular, that in 1978 the National

Commission on Uniform State Laws approved the *Uniform Audio-Visual Deposition Act*. It allows video to be used to record depositions, provided that the subpoena or any notice of the deposition specifically states that it will be taped. According to the act, any party can make a stenographic record or videotape at her own expense. If a stenographic transcript is made, both it and the video count as official records. The act further requires that the videotape begin with an oral or written statement of the camera operator's name, her employer, the date, time, and place of the deposition, the case's caption, the witness's name, the party on whose behalf the witness is testifying, and any stipulations of counsel. Counsel must then be identified on camera, and an oath must be administered to the witness. The beginning and end of each tape must be announced on camera, as must the end of the testimony. The act also allows the winners of civil cases to demand that losers assume production costs for such tapes. As of 1990, only North Dakota and Minnesota had promulgated this act, but it was widely influential in the revision of state codes of civil procedure. The act marks a substantial change in courtroom protocol to accommodate motion pictures.

The Role of Social Science in Policymaking in the Technical Era of Jurisprudence

The changes in policy, courtroom infrastructure, and legal practice that began with the promotion of videotaped depositions relied on communication studies research as well as on enthymatic "media principles" for their justification. The courts preferred to base policy on "research data" (*Guidelines*) (x), rather than on principles that they did not quite trust (as indicated by the quotation marks around the phrase "media principles") in the Federal Justice Center's tract. Jurists used general knowledge about the moving image as a mere supplement to empirical, statistical accounts of reception, because they considered the social-scientific data to be more objective. In the 1970s, the operative notion of objectivity was a technical one. Legal reasoning was not to be based on common sense or speculative argument but, if at all possible, on experimentally derived statistics. Indeed, part of the attraction of motion picture evidence in this era was that it seemed to provide an objective image of truth whose veracity was, at least in part, guaranteed by scientific principles. Yet communication studies researchers used "media principles" to frame the questions the researchers posed, and as a result, the courts could not be sure that they had not derived the signifiers of objectivity rather than signifiers that objectively conveyed their signifieds.

Social scientific research into jurors' reception of videotaped depositions assumed that trials are rule-governed "communications events" (Miller and Fontes) (15) and the research began with basic questions about the use of videos in those events: Do videos hold jurors' attention as successfully as a live witness? Do jurors retain more of the facts given in black-and-white tapes of testimony than in color tapes? Does testimony on videotape incline the jury to believe a witness more than hearing her live? Are there any differences between the information conveyed by a live witness and a videotape of that same witness?

For example, two of the most cited social scientists studying motion picture evidence, Gerald R. Miller and Norman E. Fontes, used a trial concerning an automobile accident as the "stimulus" case.[2] A cast played out the trial so that it appeared as real as possible. While the trial was presented live to one group of jurors it was taped by a four-camera system. Miller and Fontes made two videos from the footage of the trial. One was a split-screen presentation that showed a full view of the courtroom from the spectators' gallery on the bottom of the screen, while the top of the screen showed a close-up of the witness on the stand and a medium shot of the examining attorney. The other tape showed the same shots one sequentially rather than simultainously. This study found no significant difference in terms of the verdict or the amount of the award between the jurors who saw the live trial and those who saw the case on either tape (73). Miller and Fontes also found that the jurors who saw the split-screen tape said they thought that the plaintiff's attorney was slightly more persuasive than those who had seen the tape that presented one view at a time, but no other differences were reported (Miller, 1979) (145). The authors speculate that the increased credibility of the plaintiff's attorney in the split-screen version might be due to the attorney's deft use of nonverbal rhetoric (144).

The "results of this study reveal no detrimental effects on juror response as a result of viewing the videotaped trial" (73). The jurors who participated in this research were enthusiastic about the videotaped trial. The authors note that, because experienced television actors played the two attorneys, their "courtroom communication skills probably exceeded those of the average trial lawyer" (73), and that all lawyers may not be as credible on videotape as they are live. The use of actors in this experiment demonstrates how "media principles" can assert themselves in the construction of experiments. Miller and Fontes's experiment assumes that actors would accurately portray participants in a trial and that their appearance on tape would be similar to the appearance of non-thespian trial participants. Such "media principles" might seem to be common sense, but, in fact, they have the status of theoretical assumptions about the semiotics of drama and the motion picture.

A subsequent experiment carried out by Miller and Fontes in which the stimulus case involved only one or two videotaped depositions, rather than an entirely taped trial, however, did not suggest the "communicative comparability" (75)—the functional equivalence—of live and video trial presentations found in the first study. It revealed that juries tend to believe taped witnesses more than live ones. Miller and Fontes argue that this effect may be due to the popularity of television news. The authors suggest that the viewers' confidence in the veracity of what broadcasters present to them as fact makes them inclined to give credence to everything the medium presents as true (75). This argument relies on assumptions about the reception of commercial television (i.e., that audiences believe the news) to interpret the results of an experiment. The authors also speculate that the use of videotaped testimony might suggest to the jurors that the witness on the tape had pressing business elsewhere, and so was an important—hence credible—person (76).

Here, we see Ferdinand de Saussure's principle that the value of a signifier—in this case the medium of video itself—is produced by all the elements with which it is used.[3] Unlike words in language (the object of Saussure's study), the value of a medium in court varies much more emphatically in contexts in which more than one medium is used. In a trial in which all the evidence and testimony are presented on tape, the medium has no particular effect on the information that it presents. It is only in relation to oral testimony, for example, that another value of video becomes apparent. The play of difference, however, does not cease once it establishes the meaning of a sign; it extends to the various contexts of the sign's iteration. The effects of such a difference can be seen in the perceived increase in credibility of the plaintiff's attorney when the trial was presented in the split-screen format in the first experiment discussed above. We will see that this effect worried judges as well as policymakers.

In Miller and Fontes's study, the mode of presenting expert witnesses had a significant effect on three variables: the credibility of the witness presented; retention of information by jurors; and the amounts awarded by jurors. These effects were complex. The plaintiff's witness proved to be more effective in getting a large award for the plaintiff when he appeared live, but the defense witness was more effective when he appeared on tape. The jury retained the testimony of the plaintiff's expert witness better when live, but there was no difference in the jury's retention of the defense witness's testimony whether live or on tape. Although the plaintiff and the plaintiff's witness were more credible when the expert appeared live, the defense was not. "Given these results," Miller and Fontes concluded, "any impact of mode of presentation is strongly tempered by the communicative characteristics of individual witnesses" (84). These results again show the differential character of the sign and remind us that when a signifier presents other signs—as do film and video—the signs presented by the second-order signifier are themselves value-producing elements. The witnesses represented on videotape become elements in the system of signs within which the value of the medium is determined, and they therefore affect its reception.

Despite these empirical findings that show the play of difference at work in the signification of video, Miller and Fontes assign a stable meaning-producing function to each of the kinds of shots allowed in videotaping depositions. The long shot personalizes the actors and shows their gestures. The medium shot focuses on one or two actors and shows their faces more prominently than in the long shot. The close-up concentrates the viewers' attention on details (153). Miller and Fontes take these shots and their meanings from Gerald Millerson's *The Technique of Television Production* and Roy Madsen's *The Impact of Film.* According to these textbooks, the types of shots and the meanings they produce are derived from an application of common sense to the techniques of television and film production rather than from any statistical analysis of viewer responses.

The Integration of Video into the Courtroom:
Beyond the Taped Deposition

Videotaped testimony is only one of several heterogeneous uses of the
moving image in courts, but its acceptance and incorporation into daily
judicial practice facilitated the acceptance of other forms of motion
picture evidence. In the 1920s, early cases involving evidentiary films
treated motion pictures as an intruder in the courtroom, in the 1970s it
was now an accepted part of trial procedure. It had been exceptional for a
trial to use motion picture evidence at all. Now trials frequently involved
multiple evidentiary motion pictures, sometimes used to contest one
another (*Field v. Omaha Standard; Haynes v. American Motors Corporation; Brewer v. Jeep Corporation*). The introduction of videotaped
depositions familiarized courts with the techniques of video production
and exhibition. Their validity was confirmed by social scientific research.
The Federal Justice Center pilot projects and Ohio's experiments with
prerecorded videotaped trials showed that the infrastructure of the
courtroom could be easily and affordably changed to facilitate the use of
video.

The press promoted videotaped testimony further. In 1973 the *New
York Times* published three articles on the use of video in courts, a year
before the Federal Justice Center established its pilot programs and
published the first edition of its *Guidelines*. A June 10 story entitled
"Filmed Depositions Urged for Courts"[4] covers the state Supreme Court
committee's recommendation to allow videotaped depositions in New
Jersey. The *Times* apparently perceived the subject as newsworthy
because the juridical use of videotape was in its first tentative stages. The
article relays the advantages of videotape—its efficiency, its presentation
of the demeanor of the witness, and its elimination of inadmissible
material. Only three short paragraphs at the end of the piece mention
possible disadvantages: that witnesses might act insincerely on tape; that
juries might put greater emphasis on video testimony; that mechanical
failure might occur; and that procuring facilities for taking a video
deposition could be difficult. There is no suspicion of videotape as a
medium and, on the whole, the article offers a favorable impression of
videotaped depositions.

Two weeks later, a June 23 story in the *Times* covered a Vermont
civil case in which all the testimony was prerecorded (Associated Press,

1973) and it emphasized the court's ability to cut out all inadmissible testimony. The videotaping was done as part of a study by the National Center for State Courts, an organization said to seek "ways of improving the nation's court process" (Associated Press, 1973). The story reported that both the judge and the jury were enthusiastic about the use of videotape, and like the first article, this too portrayed video as the future of the courtroom.

On October 7, a third story in the *Times* covered the opening of a new, technologically advanced courtroom built both for actual trials and teaching purposes at McGeorge Law School (University of the Pacific) in Sacramento, California. The courtroom was fitted with 9-inch television monitors for each juror and an evidence pedestal equipped with a video camera for the enlargement of small exhibits. The article describes the courtroom not only as a "model" facility but also as the "courtroom of the future." (In an amusing note, the article mentions that Raymond Burr, the actor who played TV lawyer Perry Mason, donated $150,000 of the funding for this TV courtroom.)[5] All three articles construct motion picture evidence as an inevitable, welcome addition to the legal system. Such optimism could not help but support the integration of all types of motion picture evidence into juridical practice. The public discourse represented by these newspaper articles made it easier for tapes to become integrated into courtroom procedure because they were treated as part of a novel but unproblematic practice.

A little more than a year after the Vermont case, the use of tapes had spread from depositions to police procedures. In December of 1974, the *Times* published a story on the use of videotaped confessions and videotaped lineups in courtrooms in the Bronx (Andelman). It showed the ease with which video went from a single use to heterogeneous applications. Both author David Andelman and Bronx District Attorney Mario Merola were enthusiastic about this new use of video. The district attorney is quoted as saying that tapes would enable a judge to tell if a confession had been coerced or if a lineup identification had followed proper procedure. While a videotaped confession could be regarded as a form of testimony, the use of tape to determine whether the confession was forced was something new. By the same token, a videotaped lineup cannot be reduced to the same practice as a taped deposition. These particular developments do not get much attention from the article as such; rather, they are covered as part of the increasing courtroom use of

videotape in general. This is striking inasmuch as the videotaped confession and lineup not only form part of the courts' assimilation of
motion pictures but also the conversion of the police into a video-making
institution. Because of the close relationship between the courts and the
police—particularly around questions of evidence—the diffusion of
evidentiary video spread both within the juridical sphere and across
institutional boundaries.

After 1974, there was a sharp decline in the number of articles the
Times published about motion pictures in court, a lull that continued
until the end of 1978, when the issue resurfaced as part of the coverage of
the Abscam case.[6] The absence of articles about film and video evidence
over those four years can itself be read as a sign of its un-newsworthy
(hence unproblematic) status in the public sphere. Popular discourse in
this period held that it was self-evident that motion pictures were a
desirable and reliable form of evidence.

The courts did not set a new precedent to justify the admission of
videotape into evidence. That had been accomplished by the case law
governing the admission of evidentiary film. Those rulings construed
film as a form of motion picture, and the courts of the 1970s considered
video another variation thereof. In addition to framing video so as to be
admissible on the same basis as film, jurists saw video as a very desirable
convenience for presenting depositions and recording trials. The legal
community believed that the use of video would speed up often lengthy
and expensive jury trials. They were therefore motivated to incorporate
the medium into the infrastructure of the courts. A mode of representation for use in official court videos was established by government
organizations such as the Federal Justice Center in publications such as
the *Guidelines*. This mode of representation was, in effect, a pragmatically determined semiotic for legal moving images.

The Moving Image and Truth
in the 1970s and 1980s

After the courts had assimilated videotape, the 1970s and 1980s saw the
rhetorical surplus of videos maximized. Lawyers used photographs and
motion pictures as an appeal to the truth itself, and the courts' assimilation of video technology made the juridical framing of moving images

seem almost transparent. Video appeared as a window onto events rather than as one evidentiary medium among others. My consideration of cases involving evidentiary video starts with *Robert Thomas v. C. G. Tate Construction Company Inc.* and *U.S. v. Esmerejidado Guerrero,* cases that illustrate the new significance the courts assigned to video. The Abscam cases show the Federal Courts' interactions with a society in which video is key part of the infrastructure of major institutions and the willingness of that court to allow law enforcement organizations to become video producers. Abscam brings together three video-producing institutions in their most developed form: the courts, commercial television, and the police. The interweaving of each of these organizations with moving images produces the very fabric of the society of the image.

In 1979, Judge Robert H. Hemphill (United States District Court, Spartanburg, North Carolina) set out conditions under which motion pictures could be ruled inadmissible. His opinion in *Thomas v. Tate* illustrates the acceptance of evidentiary video.[7] The plaintiff, Robert Thomas, brought suit against C.G. Tate Construction Company over a car crash that left him with serious burns. On a motion in *limine* [8] to bar Thomas from showing either a videotape of one of his physical therapy sessions or some photographs of his injuries, Hemphill ruled that although the photographs were admissible, the tape was too inflammatory to be entered into evidence.

The judge's reasoning about the issue of prejudice in this case delineates the framework within which jurists of this period determined whether a film or a video was admissible evidence. Hemphill's consideration of the tape begins with an acknowledgment of the general principle that motion pictures are admissible in court—provided that they are relevant and properly authenticated. As was typical in this period, Hemphill refers to this principle without citing any particular precedent. Hemphill then spells out rule 403 of the *Federal Rules of Evidence,* which holds that relevant evidence might be excluded if it is more prejudicial than it is probative of fact in the matter before the court.[9] He reviews the precedent for the exclusion of motion pictures as prejudicial and finds that no general principle has been established to determine when motion pictures are admissible and when they ought to be excluded as inflammatory. (Each moving image offered to the courts must be entered into evidence or excluded on the basis of a review of its particular merits. Hemphill's position on applying rule 403 to films and videos became the prevalent one in this era. Instead of trying to develop a set of criteria defining an unfairly prejudicial motion picture, the courts today review each case individually.)

Hemphill's finding that determining whether or not a motion picture is unfairly prejudicial is something that must proceed on a case-by-case basis decisively reframed motion picture evidence. Despite Hemphill's reservations about the tape in the case at hand, his decision made tapes much easier to admit and enhanced their rhetorical power. From the late 1970s on, the courts treated moving images under the rubrics of several distinct types of evidence, an approach necessitated by the diffusion of videotape into various types of trial practices. To a certain extent, the courts had always made such distinctions, but now the unity of the notion of motion picture evidence itself seemed to fragment. Motion picture evidence now appeared as an open set of particulars rather than as a homogeneous category, and it was up to the courts to decide which films and videos were admissible under which conditions.

Hemphill's finding that "no prior case...could be considered controlling" in determining whether a motion picture was prejudicial is part of the deconstruction that the law tends to undergo. Juridical judgments about procedure are supposed to be based on general principles that are derived from the practice of the law. However, judicial situations arise that are ungovernable by general principle. Such situations call for improvisation, or, in legal terms, the discretion of the court. In these situations, the problem of determining whether a motion picture was prejudicial exemplifies how such improvisation occurs: motion picture evidence as a category could no longer be subjected to a general test for prejudice because moving pictures were now being used to present too many things in too many ways.

The judicial discretion here applied to the admissibility of motion pictures is not arbitrary but, rather, is an improvisation limited by legal principles and a particular situation. The court's evaluation of the risk of unfair prejudice for each piece of motion picture evidence is not outside the law but along the edges of its frame—a frame that those decisions constitute. The courts' departure from a search for a general principle in favor of decisions based on each case allowed courts to control their own procedure at the moment they arrived at the limit of the formal mode of their thought. This limit constitutes the juridical frame. and when the courts arrive at this limit, the system evolves by reframing itself.

Hemphill's opinion actually straddles two eras of motion picture evidence. Although his conclusion that films and videos must be admitted or excluded on an individual basis characterizes the emerging framing of evidentiary video, other sections of his opinion are more in line with the court's pervious attitude that expresses apprehension about such evidence. Even as late as 1979, courts were still adapting to the use of videotape. Hemphill indicates his relative unfamiliarity with motion picture evidence in a footnote stating that he recorded his impressions of the videotape on a dictaphone immediately after watching the tape, as if he were uncertain about the mechanics of watching and ruling on the tape and felt that his decision should be based on the thoughts he had during the screening .

Like the judges who first considered film evidence, Hemphill focuses on the prejudicial impact of the medium itself as well as on its content. He worried that "the novelty of using a videotape in the court-room itself may make the tape stand out in the minds of the jurors . . . The court can conceive of no way that the defendant can possibly depict with equal impact the periods of time during the plaintiff's recovery when he was either free from pain or relatively free from pain" (*Thomas v. C.G. Tate Construction Co. Inc.*) (571). The judge was concerned that, in a situation in which oral testimony and videotape contest each other, the jury will give greater weight to the video. Like Miller and Fontes, he was concerned about the value that the motion picture acquires when it is interpreted in a context that includes evidence presented through other media. Such differential significance of media themselves, rather than their contents, is a general concern.

Hemphill's main worry was the novelty, or unfamiliarity, of videotape as a means of conveying evidence. He admitted the color photographs taken at Thomas's physical therapy sessions as evidence because the medium of photography was familiar. The question of the defense's ability to present photographs of the wounds in a better light did not arise in the opinion, and we may assume from this that the tape would stand out over oral testimony in the jurors' minds more because it is an unfamiliar form of evidence than because it is pictorial.

One of the factors in Hemphill's decision to exclude the videotape was that the pain and suffering depicted on the tape was sufficiently tes-tified to by the patient's doctor, his therapist, and his wife. Hemphill found the tape, as *Federal Rules of Evidence* 403 puts it, merely "cumulative."

Presenting Thomas's pain and suffering to the court through the witnesses' testimony would eliminate the problem of how the defense could present anything that would stay in the jurors' minds as powerfully as the images on the videotape. Like other judges, Hemphill framed the notion of "fact" in such a way that both visual and spoken communication was able to convey it; whichever medium has the least affect attending it can be selected. His finding—that the tape should be excluded because it was more forceful than oral testimony—was based on a determination that motion pictures tend to produce stronger emotions and are more connotative of truth than witnesses' testimony when both types of evidence are in play.

Hemphill ruled that this tape was inflammatory because he experienced the welling-up of affect. He described the images on Thomas's tape as unusually graphic: "During the viewing of this tape one has a tendency to disregard it and direct his attention to something more pleasant, and if one has the slightest tendency to be squeamish, a feeling of nausea arises" (569). Although it seems contradictory that a lawyer would want to present an exhibit so disturbing that one has a tendency to turn away from it, such a tactic appeals to the most powerful feature of photographic and motion picture evidence. The tape creates the impression of something horrible and real that detaches itself from the specific image and cannot be controlled by the juridical frame, while the indexicality of the medium makes such an image convincing. Such a tape presents an impression of truth that is inseparable from affect and strongly persuasive. Earlier courts had found that "moving pictures present a fertile field for exaggeration of any motion or action" (*Gibson v. Gunn*) (20) and that "it is a matter of common knowledge that pictures showing a person in action may be made very deceptive by the operator of the machine used in taking the pictures" (*Massachusetts Bonding & Ins. Co. v. Worthy*) (393). These findings against motion pictures were made on the grounds that motion pictures would convince jurors of a fact whether or not they really showed one. Over the five decades following the introduction of celluloid evidence to the courtroom, between the 1920s and 1960s, such findings became less and less frequent until by the late 1970s, jurists' suspicions had turned into confidence.

The increasing variety of such evidence introduced in trials motivated the reframing of evidentiary moving images. This variety made the category "video evidence" too diffuse to be useful. The evaluation of particular videos was combined with a reduction of concern about the possible prejudice engendered by films and videos in general. The courts themselves had wanted to use video as a way of recording testimony and they had framed it as an objective medium. This new attitude made it very hard to caution against the connotations of veracity attributed to films and videos merely by virtue of their being films and videos. As a result, the surplus effects of motion picture evidence became more pronounced in this period.

Jurists had long figured ontological links between film and the world in their arguments about motion picture evidence. In the 1980s, that rhetoric was so powerful that presenting motion picture evidence had come to connote having the truth on one's side. Even if a motion picture was not a direct image of a fact at issue in a case, such images could be used to make such a fact more or less likely. However, videos were not merely links among others along a chain of inferences; case law had interpreted their semantic structure as a connection between inferences and reality.

The enthusiastic interpretation of motion picture evidence as a window on events is clear in Judge William E. Doyle's 1981 opinion in the case of *U.S. v. Guerrero*. Esmerejidado Guerrero was tried in federal court in Colorado for throwing two eggs at presidential candidate John B. Anderson during a campaign rally in Denver. News footage showed the eggs coming toward Anderson from Guerrero's direction and the subsequent pursuit of Guerrero by a police officer and members of the Secret Service. The trial judge ruled that the tape was admissible over the defense's objections that the video was unfairly prejudicial. Guerrero was convicted of assault on a member of Congress. In their appeal in the U. S. Court of Appeals Tenth Circuit, Guerrero's attorneys argued that the videotape should not have been admitted because it does not show their client in the act of egg-hurling.

In his opinion, Doyle wrote that the videotape used in the case was "the answer to a prosecutor's dream" (*United States of America v. Guerrero*) (867). Doyle ruled that any harm caused by the presentation of the tape was mitigated by the testimony of a witness who testified to having seen Guerrero throw the eggs. The video was the supreme form of evidence, and what could not be seen therein was adequately presented by oral testimony. This illustrates the ease with which the court could overcome the difference between the spoken and the seen in order to account for what lay outside the video's frame. Vision, in the form of the videotape, has taken the place of speech in the hierarchy of evidence. Yet in this case, speech came to confirm sight to mitigate any prejudice that the seeing might have caused. This was a structural possibility of the juridical reconceptualization of testimony and motion picture evidence in this period: spoken testimony provided the facts that place moving images in the context of the case, in this case facts about the off-screen physical context. Testimony supported the moving image while disappearing behind it, like the backing of a frame. Courts reduced both spoken testimony and evidentiary motion pictures to abstract facts through this process, stripping the former of its orality and the latter of its opticality.

The Guerrero tape's credibility was further bolstered by the fact that it was shot by a disinterested third party; questions about the authenticity of the tape did not arise. The judge's opinion treats the tape as a technical marvel in the service of the law. It framed the tape as a window onto the facts—the dominant juridical view of motion pictures in this period.[10] It is not incidental that, in this case exemplifying the arrival of electronic culture in the courtroom, the Guererro video came from broadcast television—one of the driving forces in the dissemination of that culture.

Doyle treated the tape as if it showed Guerrero's crime immediately and incontrovertibly. Yet the taped image merely suggests Guerrero's guilt. The crime itself is out of frame. For the tape to support the finding that Guerrero threw the eggs, the tape had to be entered into a chain of inferences by means of an argument based on facts established in the examination of witnesses. The moving image did not connect the inferences to the event in question; rather, it was connected to that event by testimony. By showing the video, the prosecution endowed the oral testimony with the power of an indexical sign by linking it to the video's suasional surplus. Once motion pictures are constituted as an index of the real, they can also function to suggest a fact rather than showing that fact directly.

Because the image does not directly show Guererro in the act of pelting Anderson, it exposes the relation between the seen and the unseen in the juridical use of motion picture evidence, as well as the porous border between sight and speech in the courts. The long-standing habit of associating the photographic image with the truth allows such images to be used convincingly in arguments for what it does not show.[11] The tape lent support to the testimony in part because of the inferences that could be made about the facts as conveyed by the tape: e.g., it showed that the eggs could have been thrown by Guerrero. However, of equal importance to the tape's persuasive role is the association of videotape with the truth. Because appearance, truth, and mechanical recordings of appearance and truth are so closely linked, the videotape was convincing to Doyle precisely because it was a videotape. His tone celebrates the very possibility of video evidence.

The chain of inferences that must be made to connect the taped image to the Guerrero-as-pelter conclusion seemed so obvious to Doyle that he did not review it in his opinion. As the court's trust in motion pictures increased, so did the rhetorical power of moving images. In this case the displacement between what the image showed and the argument within which it was used was very slight.

The power of the tape to convince the jury that Guerrero threw the eggs is its truth effect. Although the tape seems to be a primary piece of evidence, its veracity depends on its authentication by witness testimony and is supplemented by testimony about something the tape didn't show. When the tape is presented in support of such testimony, it is taken as an objective confirmation of that testimony. In motion picture evidence we see not only the court's drive to objectivity but also the conflation of the objective with the visible—and with the true.

Guerrero's defense attorneys objected that the use of the news footage by the prosecution unfairly prejudiced the jury against Guerrero. They argued that the tape was prejudicial not because it was videotape but because what could be inferred from it was not as weighty as the emotional effect that it might have on the jury. In other words, they argued that the sight of eggs coming at the congressman from Guerrero's direction would convince the jury of his guilt without logically demonstrating it. This objection revolves around the concern that the image was being used for its persuasive supplement rather than for its probative value. Doyle ruled that the witness's testimony rendered such an objection unsustainably weak. This may seem plausible *prima facie*. However, recalling Hemphill's ruling in *Thomas v. Tate*, it is remarkable that Doyle opted not to rule that the lower court was in error for admitting the Guerrero videotape, since—aside from being prejudicial—he felt that the videotape had a cumulative effect with respect to the testimony of the witness, adding no facts concerning the crime with which the defendant was charged. Doyle's opinion demonstrates a shift in the juridical valuation of such material: a re-marking of the boundaries of evidence (and thus the boundaries of the objective, the real, and the true) indicative of the court's eagerness in this period to admit motion picture evidence.

The integration of motion picture evidence into courtroom practice is marked in case law by a decline in citations of precedent to justify its admissibility. As the courts accepted video as a form of evidence and became familiar with them, judges felt that the grounds for admitting them were obvious. Appellate judges had previously reviewed decisions about the admissibility of motion picture evidence in the sections of their opinions dealing with objections to the admission of films or videos. By the mid-1970s, judges merely noted that it had been established that motion pictures were admissible as evidence, without troubling to cite any particular precedent (e.g., *Brewer v. Jeep Corporation; Field v. Omaha Standard*). The logic of objections to motion picture evidence became as diffuse as the number of legal practices in which such evidence was used: when an appellant took exception to the admission of film or video, the courts addressed the admissibility of that particular moving image without first considering the admissibility of motion picture evidence in general.

Jurists' familiarity with film and video had allayed fears that what a motion picture showed could be easily and persuasively falsified. The procedure of using the testimony of an eyewitness to authenticate motion pictures had been based on the model of authentication for photographs. Following the precedent of photographic evidence, judges wrote about film and video as consisting of a medium and content.[12] Courts now focused on the content of motion picture evidence rather than on the formal characteristics of the moving image media.

Opinions written in this period took as their dominant theme an assessment of whether what was shown by a film or video was appropriate to the particular case being tried, repressing the question of the technical means by which an image was shown. In part, this shift responded to the kinds of objections being raised; but it was also a result of framing motion picture evidence as consisting of medium and content. Attorneys recognized that the admissibility of motion pictures in general was established. So, instead of objecting to the fact that evidence took the form of videos, they now sought to exclude videos on the grounds that they depicted inadmissible images. Sometimes such objections included an argument about the effects of the motion picture apparatus on the image being presented. For example, an attorney might object to a video because the lens with which it was shot foreshortens perspective. Such arguments, however, were now made in the context of the particular image being discussed. Although the formal characteristics of a motion picture might be excluded, the motion picture as a form of evidence had become admissible in principle.

Abscam: The Apotheosis of Motion Picture Evidence

One of the most famous examples of evidentiary videotape is the Federal Bureau of Investigation's 1978 Abscam investigation and the trials that ensued. A federal judge wrote in his opinion on the appeal of one Abscam conviction that "one of the many noteworthy aspects of the Abscam investigation was the FBI's extensive use of audio and video recording equipment to create a record of conversations between Abscam operatives and individuals under investigation" (*United States of America v. Weisz et al.*). With the Abscam cases, the courts began to deal with evidence gathered by the state using advanced electronic technology—a step beyond the use of video to record confessions and lineups. Abscam was a set of cases saturated with motion pictures produced by the police and treated with absolute confidence by the courts, broadcast television, and the press. It signaled the full emergence of a society of the image.

In 1978, Abscam began as an investigation into missing art and securities. To infiltrate criminal organizations involved in the apparent thefts, the FBI set up a fictitious corporation, "Abdul Enterprises," operating as if it represented the interests of a pair of wealthy Arab businessmen. Soon after it was incorporated, Abdul Enterprises was contacted by Angelo Errichetti, mayor of Camden, New Jersey. When it became apparent to the FBI agents running Abscam that Errichetti was corrupt, the focus of Abscam shifted to political corruption and the infiltration of legitimate businesses by organized crime.

From the beginning of their investigation into Errichetti, the FBI deployed *mise en scène*. A meeting between federal agents and the mayor was arranged on "the company yacht" in Florida, a location chosen to allay any suspicions Errichetti may have had that Abdul Enterprises might be a police front by presenting him with an opulent cover. There, Errichetti was told that the "company's owners" wanted to become permanent residents of the United States. Errichetti said that he could facilitate the immigration process—in return for a fee. Errichetti introduced the FBI agents to Congressman Michael Myers, who promised to assist the "owners" of Abdul Enterprises in exchange for $50,000. Unbeknownst to Myers, the deal was videotaped, and he was charged with accepting a bribe. Abscam continued to use this asylum scenario for some time, videotaping each step in arranging the bribes. Federal prosecutors used the tapes to leverage guilty pleas; if the defendants pled innocent, the tapes were entered into evidence.

Almost every contact between Abdul Enterprises and the subjects of the Abscam investigation was recorded on audio or videotape. The FBI became a motion picture producer: it had to set up scenes—like on the yacht in Florida—that seemed realistic to the suspects. In other words, to produce tapes that clearly showed the criminal acts, the FBI had to produce a certain staging without letting the suspects know that they were being directed.

An examination of the case of *United States v. Weisz and Ciuzio* reveals in greater detail the problems Abscam faced in producing motion picture evidence. Stanley Weisz and Eugene Ciuzio set up a deal between Abdul Enterprises and Congressman Richard Kelly of Florida. Abdul Enterprises was to pay Kelly, Weisz, and Ciuzio a total of $250,000 in exchange for Kelly's promise to introduce legislation that would help the Abdul enterprises fictional owners become permanent residents of the United States. Ciuzio initially wanted all the money to be handled by Weisz, but the FBI wanted to make a tape showing the congressman being bribed. To provide the clearest evidence against Kelly, the videotape would have to show him with the bribe money and make it explicit that he was taking it in exchange for his help in allowing the heads of Abdul Enterprises to stay in the country. The videotape of Kelly accepting the bribe shows long deliberations about who should collect the money. The FBI agents posing as Abdul Enterprises executives finally convinced Kelly to take the money himself so as to avoid witnesses. To get the congressman to incriminate himself on tape, the agents claimed that they were under orders from their employers to deal with Kelly directly and to get his word on the matter. Kelly agreed to take the first $25,000 himself and promised that he would help the bosses of Abdul Enterprises. Kelly had not brought a briefcase in which to carry the money because he anticipated having one of his associates collect it, but he appeared on tape putting the cash into his pockets.

Weisz and Ciuzio each took exception to the admission of the videotape evidence in the appeal of their convictions submitted to Justice George E. McKinnon of the District Court of the District of Columbia in 1983. The main argument in the early 1980s against the admission of the videotapes was that they prejudiced the jury—in this case on the grounds that the mere sight of a congressman stuffing $25,000 into his pockets would inflame ordinary citizens. Ciuzio wanted to suppress the entire tape, while Weisz asked that the section showing Kelly pocketing the money be edited. The editing of such tapes was a matter for negotiation between the interested parties and the court.

Along with asking that the tape be excluded as prejudicial, Ciuzio argued that the tape showed that the congressman was unprepared to receive a bribe—suggesting lack of foreknowledge—and there was thus an absence of a conspiracy. Kelly had not brought a container for the money, and Ciuzio said that if he had known the congressman would be given a bribe, he would have brought a briefcase for Kelly's convenience. Ciuzio used the fact that he had not done so as evidence of the congressman's lack of knowledge regarding what was happening.

Ciuzio argued that the tape of the congressman loading up with cash was sufficiently prejudicial to suppress the entire tape, and furthermore —in a seemingly discordant second argument—that the tape demonstrated the absence of a conspiracy and was thus exculpatory evidence. These two arguments were an attempt to cover all bases: the tape would be improper to show in an attempt to obtain a conviction, but a showing of it would countervail the conspiracy charge. These claims show that the arguments made by lawyers were *ad hoc* and determined by pragmatic considerations rather than an overarching logic.[13]

The trial court said that "to see a congressman stuffing any amount of money into his pockets is a disgusting, revolting sight" (*United States of America v. Weisz and Cuizio*) (431); it agreed that such an image was potentially prejudicial. Nonetheless, the court allowed the entire tape to be shown to the jury, holding the view that it added nothing to the government's case. This decision was supported in the ruling on the defendants' motion for retrial, in which the McKinnon held that the trial court's decision was well within its discretion. The complete integration of video is demonstrated by the court's simultaneous admission that the tape added nothing to the case and its failure to find it cumulative.

In his opinion, McKinnon wrote that the tape provided direct evidence of Kelly's relationship with Ciuzio, both when it showed Kelly asking to talk privately with Ciuzio and when Kelly stated that the financial dealings should go through Ciuzio. In other words, Kelly's familiarity with the proposal for the investments shows that Ciuzio had briefed him. Furthermore, McKinnon wrote that, the tape provided "irrefutable evidence that Kelly had, in fact, been bribed," and so provided a necessary element in proving the charges of aiding and abetting brought against Weisz and Ciuzio.

The judge's view that the tape provides irrefutable evidence is typical of the attitude of the judiciary toward motion picture evidence in this period; as in *United States v. Guerrero*, videotape was held to be a transparent depiction of the truth. Although McKinnon agreed that the sight of Kelly stuffing money into his own pockets was prejudicial, he pointed out that for evidence to be excluded under Rule 403 it must be *unfairly* prejudicial. Insofar as the tape shows the very crime that Weisz and Ciuzio are accused of, aiding and abetting, it is not unfairly so.

McKinnon also finds that the prejudicial effect of the tape was further ameliorated because prospective jurors in the case were asked during the *voir dire* hearing—the phase of the trial in which jurors are selected—if the sight of a congressman stuffing $25,000 into his pockets would make them find everyone involved guilty. Those who answered yes were excluded for cause (*United States of America v. Weisz and Cuizio*). This finding shows that by 1983 motion picture evidence had become so familiar that lawyers were selecting jurors on the basis of their potential reactions to videos. As the use of films and tapes became increasingly common in courtrooms, they began to affect every phase of the trial process.

In the case under discussion, Ciuzio also argued that the video and audio recordings of people other than himself and Wiesz—the parties on trial—should be excluded as hearsay. Under *Federal Rule of Evidence* 801(d)(2e), hearsay is admissible in a case in which there is evidence of a conspiracy. Ciuzio tried to argue that there was no such evidence. The court admitted the recordings, finding that the government had shown some continuity of purpose among Ciuzio, Kelly, Wiesz, and others as required under 801(d)(2e). On appeal, Ciuzio argued that the rule requires that the common purpose shared by members of the conspiracy be unlawful; McKinnon found that claim to be false, opining that the rule requires only that numerous parties be acting together for a common goal.

Abscam received extensive press coverage. Articles in the *New York Times* cast the tapes as incontrovertible proof of guilt. In interviews, legal experts said that there was no realistic possibility of using entrapment as a defense. When the cases were adjudicated, television news programs broadcast many of the tapes as proof of the corruption of members of congress. The use of these tapes on television adds a stream of images running from the courts through the rest of the public sphere, a flow historically antinomial to the evidentiary use of news footage (as in the *United States of America v. Guerrero*).

Changes in Technology, Changes in Practice

The assimilation of motion pictures into the juridical sphere was not marked by the adoption of a completely developed, unchanging technology by an institution with unyielding rules. The original pilot video programs set up by the Federal Justice Center that used black-and-white cameras together with studies that indicated that jurors retained more information from a black-and-white tape than from a color tape gave way by the 1980s to a preference for color tapes. Color cameras were the commercial standard while black-and-white cameras were almost impossible to find. Additionally, new color video cameras did not require the intense lighting that the older models did. This technological change brought with it a semiotic change. Attorneys argued that "the use of black-and-white recording for litigation should be considered as inherently inflammatory because of the somber feeling attached to such images" (Heller, 1987). Video technology rapidly transformed from the 1970s through the 1990s, and the changes produced variations in the semiopragmatics of evidentiary motion pictures.

Once again, difference can be seen driving the production of meaning. When monochrome and color video were both familiar forms to jurors, and the courts assumed that either mode was suitable to convey information, the courts preferred black-and-white video for its reputed quality of helping jurors retain information. When black-and-white became almost obsolete in mainstream television and cinema production, it ceased to be a transparent mode of recording. It became unusual and hence problematic.

As motion picture technology saturated the juridical sphere, its framework changed such that it no longer appeared novel and in need of justification. Instead, its use appeared as an obvious element of legal practice. The integration of video into courtroom practice is marked by the ways in which continuing education handbooks for lawyers, published within a few years of each other in 1983 and 1987, present arguments for the admission of such evidence. These arguments are of great semiopragmatic importance: they show that the 1980s began with video conditioned by a connotation of novelty and thus in need of justification, and ended with video conditioned by a connotation of familiarity to the point that its exclusion needed to be justified. As the 1980s progressed, these arguments became more self-confident until they became so perfunctory as to imply that it was unnecessary to argue for the inclusion of a film or video with any but the most procedurally conservative of judges.

Video Techniques in Trial and Pretrial, a handbook for lawyers, published in 1983, contains a chapter by John Buchanan, Carol Bos, and Fred Heller on the admissibility of videotaped evidence. The main part of this chapter takes the form of a mock judicial opinion, written from the point of view of a judge who is a proponent of the use of motion picture evidence. The opinion traces the precedent for admitting motion pictures into evidence as far back as 1941. It considers an irreducible diversity of uses of videotape: to present experiments, to present accident reconstructions, to present events at issue in a case, and to illustrate the opinion of an expert witness. It also considers cases in which the tape has been edited. The authors lay out case law to be used to persuade judges to admit videotapes into evidence. The research into the precedent for each type of motion picture evidence indicates that the authors felt such arguments might be useful to their readers, presumably because, at the time of publication, attempts to exclude videotape on the grounds that the medium itself was objectionable were still common.

In 1987, Fred Heller published *Advanced Litigation Skills Using Video,* another collection of texts to accompany a continuing education seminar. The same article that he co-authored on admissibility from the 1983 volume is reprinted here in slightly revised form. The additions to the article mainly take into account new decisions favoring the admission of videotapes. The chapter also takes a more strident tone in discussing the validity of motion picture evidence. Earlier sections of the handbook, in two summary statements, deal with the issue of how to introduce videos into evidence. The first informs the reader that case law supporting the admissibility of motion pictures goes back to 1881 with the case of *Cowley v. New York*, in which the judge found that photographs are admissible under the same principle that permits paintings to be used as evidence if they are supported by other testimony (Heller, 1987). According to Heller, this same principle applies to videotapes, which in general are held to be admissible so long as they are supported by a witness's testimony that they are a fair and accurate representation of what they purport to portray. The second statement holds that the judge has the discretion to exclude motion picture evidence if its content is found to be inadmissible, but "[the judge] has no discretionary right to exclude such evidence on the basis that such evidence is inherently inadmissible" (Heller, 1987).

Handbooks on the use of motion pictures in court, including the two edited by Heller, proliferated in the 1980s as a way to educate lawyers about these new techniques. Lawyers wanted to use film and video because they believed that moving images could make juries see their side of a case more clearly than words. The introduction to *Video Techniques in Trial and Pretrial* claims that videotaped evidence can save the embattled jury system by making complex cases clear to jurors (9). *Advanced Litigation Skills Using Video* promotes the "vast potential and benefit" of video for "litigators, their clients, and the courts and juries who must decide their cases" (9). Another handbook, entitled *Modern Visual Evidence* claims that videotape keeps judges and juries interested in cases and helps them to understand what is being argued; this "in turn puts them in a position to be—and increases the likelihood that they will be—receptive to the position being urged" (Joseph, 1990). In *Video: A Guide for Lawyers*, Ellen J. Miller congratulates lawyers who were the first "on the block to be using video" for their "farsightedness" (Miller, 1983) (2).

Attorneys justified claims for the moving image's superiority over language with (often implicit) assumptions about the semiotics of each medium. However, the theories of signification found in these tracts are not the same as those informing policy. The primers construct theories of signification by speculation, only rarely referring to the social-scientific data preferred by policymakers. On the one hand, policy attempts to regulate the form of motion pictures entered into evidence and to set criteria for their authentication; on the other, the primers use the semiotics of the image to address different issues, among which are the limitations imposed on the use of evidentiary motion pictures by policy. These manuals teach lawyers how to present a motion picture to the greatest effect in a case and how to cross-examine the foundational witness[14] for a film or video. Policy and primers make different assumptions about the semiotics of motion picture evidence because they consider divergent aspects of the signification of moving images in courtroom practice.

In the first chapter of *Video Techniques in Trial and Pretrial*, Buchanan, Bos, and Heller make explicit the semiotic assumptions about speech and the moving image that underlie the promotion of motion picture evidence in such manuals. They believe that the benefits of the moving image's mode of signification are linked to the political goal of preserving the jury system. They note that the question of whether to keep the jury system "at all is a frequent topic of conversation in legal circles" (Heller, 1983). Critics complain that jury trials are long and expensive and that the facts in many contemporary civil cases are too complex for juries to understand. Instead of eliminating the jury, they suggest using videotape to expedite trials and make complex situations more readily comprehensible (10).

According to Buchanan, Bos, and Heller, video would accomplish these goals because of its capacity to communicate certain things more precisely than language. The authors believe videotaped testimony is always superior to oral or written testimony because it reduces the "gap between communication and understanding" and thus helps to reduce "uncertainty and anxiety" (91). As with judicial opinions and policy, the manuals tend to hold that motion picture evidence is composed of medium and content. In addition, like the opinion and policy discourses, *Video Techniques in Trial and Pretrial* portrays video as a transparent medium that presents a highly focused content. The authors contend that oral testimony consists of "mere words" that "leave much to the imagination of the listener, based upon his or her own experience" (Heller, 1983) (10).

Their theory is that the meaning of language is produced by reference to a private, interior lexicon. Variations in the ways people understand words result in an unacceptable degree of polysemy in testimony—"to understand any verbal communication, the individual jurors will naturally interrelate their own understanding of a concept" (Heller, 1983) (10). Buchanan, Bos, and Heller claim that asking ten people to define the word "house" will produce ten different meanings. In this text the implicit critique that video brings to a tradition of jurisprudence based on oral testimony is made explicit by arguing that the evidentiary video circulates a sight objectively that all of the jurors see for themselves *in the same way*.

Buchanan, Bos, and Heller further argue that photographs restrict language's ambiguity of meaning. They write that "a photograph, while open to some subjective interpretation, greatly reduces differences in overall comprehension" (10). By reducing the polysemy of oral testimony, photographic evidence affords attorneys a greater degree of precision in communicating their arguments. The authors go on to write that "the old saying that 'a picture is worth a thousand words' is especially true in a trial setting. You have to be absolutely sure that the jury understands the message, exactly as you intended them to" (10). If photography represents a step toward such exactitude, video is an even bigger improvement: it presents not just one image but a series of "electronic pictures" at the rate of "thirty a second" (11).

Whereas policymakers tend to use the live witness as the standard against which any other forms of evidence are to be judged, Buchanan, Bos, and Heller use videotape as a means of rectifying the shortcomings of live oral testimony. The authors present motion pictures as a reproduction of a presence against which the truth of oral testimony can be gauged. When photographs and motion pictures were first introduced into courtrooms, jurists were suspicious of them and allowed them to be used only as a means of illustrating oral testimony. Motion pictures displace speech from the head of the evidentiary hierarchy by obviating the need to interpret language. Elsewhere the authors write that video, not testimony, "is the next best thing to witnessing a live occurrence" (9). Despite such enthusiasm for evidentiary video, oral testimony was still necessary to authenticate motion picture evidence, and the tension between the oral and visual modes of evidence opens the same structure screened by the logic of video and testimony in *United States v. Guerrero*.

Buchanan, Bos, and Heller contend that motion picture evidence saves time and money by expediting trials while—by eliminating the ambiguity of language—it enables jurors to comprehend what would otherwise be beyond their ken. The authors conclude that motion picture evidence is the best means of preserving the jury system, which they assert is the surest way to a fair trial because it appeals to "collective common sense and feelings of duty to carefully weigh the evidence" and cancels out individual bias (10).

The assertion that the use of videotaped evidence is a means of preserving the jury system is common to many of the primers on courtroom use of moving images.[15] They all present motion pictures as an improved means of communicating with the jury. The handbooks are careful to cast motion picture evidence as fundamentally objective, while at the same time explicitly recommending that the *appearance* of objectivity be used to sway the jury (or the judge) in favor of the party offering the moving image into evidence. They attempt to use the persuasive supplement that had so concerned jurists of a previous era. Although policy and case law attempt to ensure that motion pictures are used to communicate objective facts, manuals for lawyers present strategies for taking advantage of the suasional surplus and the truth effects generated by films and videos.

The handbooks present tactics for taking advantage of the rhetorical force of video evidence when considering uses of the technologies that are not directly addressed by policy. The videotaped deposition is the subject of numerous policy documents because it serves as an official recording produced by a court officer. However, other kinds of tapes are not so elaborately regulated: documentary tapes that present, for example, a day in the life of a plaintiff handicapped by an injurious incident or accident, a taped experiment, or a serendipitous recording of events at issue in the case.

The handbooks also evince an excitement about the use of videotape in court when describing recommended forms and production procedures. These techniques are meant to be exciting to judges and juries as well as to the lawyers using them since, as *Modern Visual Evidence* puts it, "the principal nemesis of any trial lawyer is not so much his adversary as boredom on the part of the fact finder" (Joseph, 1990) (2). Although they are careful to distinguish between motion picture evidence and other uses of the moving image, the handbooks sometimes gleefully invoke examples from commercial motion picture production to explain production procedures. Excitement over the use of motion pictures is palpable in a chapter in *Advanced Litigation Skills Using Video* on how to videotape a deposition. Additionally, Buchanan, Bos, and Heller emphasize the importance of where a deposition is shot. In doing so, they take recourse in an example from commercial media production. "Cecil B. DeMille, one of the greatest movie producers of all time, shot most of his breathtaking 'outdoor' action scenes inside" because the studio "gave film makers complete control over their filming environment" (Heller, 1987) (71). They recommend that attorneys use an equally controlled (if smaller) space to record depositions. The authors continue "'camera, lights, action—quiet on the set' are still appropriate terms to the people involved in this work. Planning a videotape deposition, like making a major motion picture, requires utmost attention to all environmental considerations that affect the quality of the production" (Heller, 1987) (72).

Because of their familiarity to the general public, commercial film and television serve as a background against which the use and production of motion picture evidence is explained. In the passage about DeMille in *Advanced Litigation Skills Using Video*, the authors' thrill at being involved in motion picture production is legible. The background of commercial media production is used to give form to motion picture evidence. In policy documents and the shot lists of the handbooks, it is used as a horizon against which the meanings of shots are produced. In *Advanced Litigation Skills Using Video*, the reference to Hollywood production techniques explains how the technology should be used for best results. Miller and Fontes use both the popularity and credibility of television news to explain the legitimizing effect of the videotape deposition on the testimony it communicates.

At the same time, these handbooks are careful to note that the aura of commercial production must not overwhelm juries and judges. Attorneys' desire to produce tapes that impress the jury with their objectivity leads to a concern in the handbooks about the reception of such tapes by juries. In another chapter of *Advanced Litigation Skills Using Video*, Fred and Lynn Heller seek to ensure a favorable jury reaction to evidentiary tapes by emphasizing the criterion of "good taste" (Heller, 1987) (27). They write that good taste "relates to the concept that nudity, personal hygiene procedures, or other events which may be potentially embarrassing to either the viewer or the participant need not be recorded in their entirety" (27). Another chapter explains that exaggeration in a day-in-the-life video can "neutralize the injury and anaesthetize the viewer. He becomes used to the injury; it doesn't take very long before the viewer actually begins to feel uncomfortable about the situation" (92). The authors offer the example of a scene in which a plaintiff with a nerve injury struggles to get peas into his mouth with a fork, which might produce "such negative viewer response that those who watch the scene become upset that it was even included. There are other more tasteful ways of demonstrating nerve damage" (91).

In this way the Hellers warn that scenes in bad taste alienate jurors. They also argue that any such scenes ought to be ruled inflammatory and inadmissible. That the criterion of good taste is applied to motion picture evidence indicates an anxiety inside the legal community that the moving image is a potentially vulgar intruder into their sphere of activity. The primers argue that any videotaped evidence is admissible unless its content is objectionable, since such tapes are merely a way of presenting evidence that might be introduced by other means.

The Hellers claim that the objectivity of typical day-in-the-life tapes of handicapped plaintiffs is self-regulating because "any lawyer who attempts to introduce into evidence a video documentary that is anything but absolutely honest and accurate runs a high risk that the evidence will backfire in a devastating way" when the foundational witness is cross-examined (Heller, 1983) (12). The authors do not, however, suggest that cross-examination is an effective way of counteracting any connotations of the editing technique and camera style of the tape. While claiming that the adversarial structure of the legal system ensures the truthfulness of such tapes, the Hellers also teach lawyers that cross-examining the foundational witness is an effective tactic in attacking tapes.

Lawyers frequently objected to edited films and videos on the grounds that the omissions and rearrangements in such evidence introduce bias. A *Trial* magazine article by Gregory Joseph, the author of *Modern Visual Evidence*, "Demonstrative Videotape Evidence," points out that the principal of Federal Rule of Evidence 1006[16] permits news broadcasts and home movies offered as evidence to be condensed, provided that the foundational testimony shows that the edited tapes were voluminous and that the summary is fair (Joseph, 1986). Any misgivings about the editing of such condensed tapes brought out by the opposing counsel are not grounds for exclusion but can be used by the jury to determine the probative weight of the tape (Joseph, 1986).

Because Rule 1006 only applies to summaries of voluminous data, it does not apply to most tapes. Another argument is needed to justify the editing of, for example, day-in-the-life tapes. The Hellers point out that editing "should not by its nature raise the specter of untruth or deception" (Heller, 1987) (22), because all evidence is edited by attorneys: the decision to offer one exhibit rather than another or the selection of questions to put to a witness exemplify for the authors editing of the same sort as cutting the moving image. To support these claims, the Hellers provide the transcript from the *Supreme Court of the State of New York v. Medical Center* for September 24, 1985, in which the defense objects to a day-in-the-life tape on the grounds that it was edited and included dissolves. The court overruled the objection.

The Hellers consider editing one of the permissible means of taking advantage of the apparent objectivity of the moving image. They also recommend the use of certain shots rather than others, to the same effect. The recommended shots, they hold, are meant to help attorneys by presenting their material persuasively while functioning as signs of the tape's objectivity. Inappropriate shots would reduce the effectiveness of a tape just as would blatantly biased editing. The authors recommend that the close-up can "concentrate interest and can draw attention to reactions, response, or emotions. The close-up can also focus attention and point out information that might otherwise have been overlooked" (20).

According to the Hellers, one of the principle uses for the close-up is to depict reactions. This seems to contradict the Federal Justice Center's *Guidelines For Pre-Recording Testimony on Videotape Prior to Trial*, which construes the reaction shot as potentially inflammatory in depositions. Nonetheless, the Hellers recommend its use in day-in-the-life tapes. They make such a recommendation not only because depositions and documentaries are different sorts of tapes but also because their goals are different from those of the Federal Justice Center. The Hellers seek to take advantage of the connotations of reaction shots without affecting the impression of objectivity generated by the tape. If a lawyer is successful in using this technique, she will have wedded the impact of the reaction shot to the tape's truth effect.

Although the Hellers advise readers that the close-up can be used to show reactions, they warn that "extreme caution should be used when analyzing the potential 'prejudicial effect' of [reaction shots]. Although reaction shots are short . . . and subtle, they may have powerful impact.

They are also usually shot at a time different from when the reaction appears to be taking place" (37). The authors worry that reaction shots might not get past a judge, and that—if they did—they could ruin the entire tape's credibility for a jury. That reaction shots could be taken at a different time from the tape's main action could be raised in cross-examination. If the foundational witness for a tape was made to say in open court that a shot taken at a later point was inserted into a tape to make it seem as though it was part of the action, the entire tape's evidentiary value might collapse under the weight of ostentation and confabulation.

This chapter of *Advanced Litigation Skills Using Video* contains a list of shots and their semiotic values. Much of this taxonomy of the moving image is derived from the use of shots in commercial motion picture production. The Hellers assert that "a camera angle in which a person is recorded from above, may make him seem small, weak, or insignificant. Recording from below may make him seem large or important" (Heller, 1987) (39) that "a rapid zoom in produces a highly dramatic thrust toward the subject conveying the impression of great significance or importance" (40); "a medium shot can also de-emphasize flaws that a close-up would reveal" (39). In making these claims, the Hellers are merely repeating the connotations assigned to shots in textbooks on television and film production.

The Hellers advise their readers that attorneys should be "very judicious" (22) when using the extreme close-up in an evidentiary videotape. They also recommend that evidentiary video makers avoid using the over-the-shoulder shot because it "verges on the 'slick'" (35). These shots are not recommended because they are marks of sophisticated production values and subjective points of view, which in turn are read as signs of bias. Under this theory—that a videotape is admissible if it is accompanied by testimony that it is a fair representation of what it pretends to be (11)—over-the-shoulder shots and extreme close-ups would be permissible unless deemed prejudicial by the judge. The Hellers are reluctant recommend their use not because of their potential inadmissibility, but because such artifice might make the jury suspicious that the tape attempted to persuade rather than merely inform them. The truth effect of motion picture evidence depends on the impression of objectivity it gives the jury. To create this impression, videotapes must avoid patently rhetorical devices.

Advanced Litigation Skills Using Video delineates a normative style for evidentiary videotape based on certain expectations of a jury's response. The recommended style includes using even, bright light (to render everything on screen fully visible), a minimum of background noise, clear images, smooth camera movements, and unobtrusive cutting. The Hellers state that proper lighting ensures "accuracy and objectivity" (73). This style is derived from the "first commandment" of making evidentiary videotape, set out in the book's first chapter: "use the medium to communicate a message, never to be a message" (11). Rendering video as a mere instrument of communication increased its suasional surplus by de-emphasizing it.

To ensure that the medium appear transparent, *Advanced Litigation Skills Using Video* recommends producing tapes displaying professional production values rather than those of a home movie. The basis for this advice is the difference between television and film: "the argument that a jury can better relate to a 'home movie' cannot be extended to videotape. As the technologies are different so are the products and their effects on the average viewer" (93). Despite the common use of camcorders to tape family events, Heller and Heller argue that in an evidentiary videotape that amateur style would call attention to itself because no one is used to "home-movie quality television" (93). Unlike home movies, video evidence ought to be "put together so that it flows in a logical sequence"; great care, they say, should be taken to ensure that the presentation is free of any technical glitches (94). Lawyers who want to use such evidence but cannot ensure the quality of the tapes themselves are advised to hire a production company specializing in the production of motion picture evidence.

Not all motion picture evidence avails itself of presentation in the normative style. For example, the probative value of serendipitous recordings of the events at issue in a trial, or of security camera footage, often mandates their use despite the absence of preferred illumination. The tactics described in the handbooks often seem to contradict each other out of the pragmatic needs of lawyers, which countermand consistency. Although *Advanced Litigation Skills Using Video* generally recommends video techniques that impress the jury with a strong sense of objectivity, Buchanan, Bos, and Heller suggest in their chapter that, in a case in which the plaintiff's double vision was caused by an accident, a tape showing the plaintiff's work environment as it now appeared to him would be effective in gaining compensation for lost wages. Such a tape might be edited, provided that the plaintiff testified that it was a fair and accurate representation of the way the world appeared to him. The tape would inevitably require the use of a special filter that would draw attention to the medium; it would also be shot from the plaintiff's subjective point of view.

Many of the handbooks argue that video is significantly better than film for use in litigation. The primers take such a position in part to reassure attorneys that video differs from film. Celluloid had a reputation for being expensive, difficult to produce, and inconvenient to exhibit; it was never fully integrated into the courts. Buchanan, Bos, and Heller write that the advantages of videotape over motion picture film include portability, resistance to environmental extremes, the ability to provide immediate feedback, and the physical integrity of the master tape, which remains uncut (Heller, 1987). In *Modern Visual Evidence*, Joseph points out that video is easier to index than film, arguing that the light does not have to be adjusted in the courtroom to show a tape, and that "it is said to be physiologically less comfortable to watch a film than tape in court because the viewers' pupils must contract and dilate to accommodate to the attendant changes in the (none too subtle) lighting" (1–8 to 1–9). He also claims that video "plays as it records—only in real time" (1–7) and that consequently it is not subject to the objection of the recording having been made at the wrong speed (1–9).

Joseph's last point as well as the contention of Buchanan, Bos, and Heller that editing film always involves cutting the original are both wrong. These claims show the authors' lack of technical knowledge. Video can be shown in slow or fast motion with the aid of an editing console equipped with a jog control. Skillful use of this device can speed up or slow down a tape without rendering the movements it depicts jumpy. Only reversal film requires the cutting of the original. When negative film is used, a print can be cut while the original negative remains intact. The ignorance of technology exhibited by these claims is important in that the authors are using assumptions about the technical qualities of the medium to make the semiotic point that video is somehow more indexical than film. Joseph argues falsely that video is an infallible reproduction of the speed of movements because it can only be shown in real time; Buchanan, Bos, and Heller argue with equal inaccuracy that an edited film is always open to the suspicion that crucial footage has been lost forever. These arguments together suggest that video is somehow a more accurate index of the state of affairs than is film. In *Modern Visual Evidence* Joseph concludes that video is a direct, inviolable record of the speed of the event recorded—of action's very relationship to time—whereas in *Advanced Litigation Skills Using Video* Buchanan, Bos, and Heller conclude that an edited film does not preserve an index of the whole event recorded. Both of these books reason from false assertions about the technical characteristics of the media; both in turn arrive at conclusions about their mode of signification.

In the period between 1970 and 1990, the courts instituted a framework that allowed them to conceptualize and use films and videos. A semiopragmatics of juridical motion pictures was produced by the competing discourses of attorneys, policymakers, judges, and public opinion. This change in the juridical superstructure was accompanied by a change in the infrastructure of the courts. Courts acquired video production and exhibition equipment. In fact, a small industry developed around the use of evidentiary videotapes so that by 1987, the National Court Reporters Association began publishing a list of video production firms for recording depositions and a list of court reporters who were certified to take video depositions. The practical application of heterogeneous uses of the motion picture engendered aporias. These aporias were in turn ignored or resolved on a case-by-case basis, depending on the contingencies of practical problems. The legal use of motion picture evidence was accompanied by the increased use of moving images throughout U.S. culture, creating a stream of technologically produced images linking all of its major institutions. In this period, the motion picture appeared in these frames as the expression of the truth in an objective, technical mode. By the early 1990s, however, the aporias opened by the use of motion picture evidence reframed the courts' use of films and videos. Their indexical connection to the real would again be under suspicion even as their use would continue.

5

The Rodney King Case, or Moving Testimony

B etween the initial use of evidentiary films in the late 1910s and the spread of evidentiary video in the 1980s, the use of moving images at trial increased steadily. Motion picture evidence became part of the cultural imaginary through newspaper accounts and films like Fritz Lang's *Fury* (1936). The images used at trial, however, largely remained in courtrooms. In 1991, George Holiday's tape of Rodney King's beating by Los Angeles police officers appeared on broadcast news and was later used in court. Although some images from evidentiary films and tapes had appeared in newspapers and on television, those images did not capture the public's imagination in the same way that the King tape did. In part this was because when images had previously been published, as in the Abscam case, they were released after the trial had begun and there was no controversy about the court's understanding of the tapes. The images appeared as accounts of an event that was already over and had ended in court. Unlike the other publicized images, the Holiday tape was broadcast before trial and became a complex cause in an ongoing event. The public responses to the tape, the two trials of the officers involved, and the uprising in LA were driven by the circulation of the video and can be thought of as an image-event.[1]

Image-events involve the circulation of an image that must be shown and which the culture cannot respond to. Various institutions show the image over and over, driven by need to see the image and the impossibility of adequately acting on it, resulting in the image's compulsive circulation.

Holiday's tape was shown on television, presented as evidence in court, used as the introductory sequence of Spike Lee's film *Malcolm X* (1992), and exhibited in the 1993 Whitney Biennial, to name only a few examples. Each showing solicits a response that it fails to receive, so the image seeks its answer somewhere else. If its screenings lead to contradictory understandings, the image-event extends itself to play out the social contradictions expressed in those understandings.

In the courts, evidentiary motion pictures and testimony grew more and more intricately connected over the history of their use. In the 1920s and 1930s the courts established that films could be shown at trial if they were properly authenticated by a witness. By the 1940s, jurists discovered that films could be framed either as physical evidence or as pictorial communication of testimony—depending on the protocol used to authenticate them. Even the formulation "pictorial communication of witness testimony" names something different from testimony itself. Neither witness testimony nor physical evidence function as proof as such. Each establishes a fact about the case used in an argument presented by one side or the other.

The 1970s and 1980s saw the integration of the moving image into the infrastructure of the courts. As the courts increasingly accepted evidentiary motion pictures, less and less testimony was required to authenticate them. Authentication only required a witness to identify the time and place where such films were taken. The court's assimilation of video technology led to a widespread acceptance of video as physical proof of an event and thus to a proliferation of the moving image as nonsubjective vision. At the same time, testimony was regularly presented in the form of videotaped depositions, and closed circuit television was used to bring the testimony of far-flung and overbooked expert witnesses into the courtroom in a timely manner. All these practices tightly weave together tapes and testimony, but none of them present video as testimonial.

Although films and videos can only appear as evidence framed by testimony, film and video also displace testimony from its position atop of the hierarchy of evidence. In the 1950s, the conflict between evidentiary hierarchies, one privileging testimony and the other visual evidence, made the situation even more complex. Evidentiary images of all kinds and witness testimony became woven together, each interpreting the other.

In the 1980s jurists came to consider video evidence as the most reliable form of evidence. The widespread use of a motion picture format that could easily be broadcast on television created the necessary conditions for a public conflict between two understandings of an image. In fact, Holiday's tape functioned differently on television and at trial. Although the same videotape could be shown at trial and broadcast, jurists and journalists work with images differently and the same videotape could appear as testimony on television and as another form of evidence at trail. In court, evidentiary videos can only be shown as part of arguments about facts at issue in the case; if they make an emotional appeal they can be excluded as prejudicial. Seen as a window onto events, and much more convenient to make and present than film, video evidence became so common that it was only a matter of time before an evidentiary video shown at trial was broadcast on television and the different uses of the tape would lead to direct social conflict.

The spread of inexpensive, portable consumer video cameras such as Handicams was a contributing factor. Such cameras made it much easier and more convenient for amateurs to make moving images. An evidentiary video produced by a private citizen is much more likely to be broadcast than one produced by the state. Litigants could delay the broadcast of the FBI's Abscam tapes through legal proceedings because the tapes were made by the FBI.

Holiday taped the March 3 beating at the suggestion of his wife, who had been awakened by sounds in the night. The next day she called the Foothill Police Station to ask about the episode but they would not tell her anything. She suggested that her husband bring it to a television station and he contacted KTLA, which broadcast it on the local news on March 4. Before airing the tape, KTLA's news staff contacted the LAPD press relations department to get an official reaction. The police could not control the exhibition of the tape, they merely responded to it by promising to investigate the incident. The Holidays initially used the tape as a means to get the state to address an abuse of its power. On March 5 it was broadcast nationally by CNN and ABC and the following night national evening news shows carried the tape.[2]

The reading of the tape by Los Angeles television audiences is well documented. On March 10, 1991, the *Los Angeles Times* published a poll showing that 92 percent of the city's residents who had seen the tape thought it showed that police had used excessive force against King. The affective force of the tape was so strong that on March 21 President George Bush told reporters that what he saw made him "sick."[3]

The public judged the image of Rodney King's beating on the basis of its affective force, a force inscribed on the surface of the tape and which, on television, served to guarantee the testimonial truth of the tape. The dark, grainy image, taken some distance from the events and so different from the other images on television meant something to television audiences, whereas, at trial, it was not considered at all. Affective judgments are considered prejudicial and not permitted in court. On television, the image was according to different rules. It was an image of a cruel beating. In court the image could only be part of an argument about the beating.

The public sense of injustice at the verdict allowed the image-event to continue and resulted in the subsequent uprising, which was sparked by the difference between the appearance of the image in television news programs and the courts that had come to figure racial injustice in the Untied States. In the courts, videotapes such as Holiday's, so-called serendipitous recordings, do not constitute testimony. They must be authenticated by testimony.[4]

The trial of the police officers who beat Rodney King (*California v. Powell, Koon, Wind and Briseno*) (1992) exposed the different ways in which television news programs and the courts frame the relationship between video and testimony. On television, tapes can appear as affective testimony to traumatic events.

The Rodney King tape became an image-event because of the difference between the courtroom and broadcast news. The courts regulate testimony in an explicit, formal manner, while on television it is defined implicitly and informally. The tele-spectator knows testimony when she sees it. Certain images on television function as testimony, even if the institution of broadcast television does not set rules for testimonial video. In fact, on television, testimonial video tends to appear as an image that breaks normal broadcasting practices.

A rigorous definition of "motion picture testimony" must take into account a shifting network of meanings constantly being reframed in the development of institutional practices and technical developments. The exhibition of Holiday's tape both on television and in court will allow me to indicate the specificity of each institution's concepts and practices of testimony, and the difference between those practices will illuminate the historical mechanism of the image-event driven by the tape.

In order to show how this is so, I will define testimonial video by referring to C. A. J. Coady's analytic definition of testimony. I will follow the definition with readings of Avital Ronnel's essay on the Rodney King tape to show how the notion of testimony works in their analyses. In general, philosophy has neglected the topic of testimony. When philosophers have attended to it, they have done so in order to dismiss it as a less reliable form of knowledge experience or thought.

Coady extrapolates his general definition of testimony from the model of formal testimony in a legal setting. Formal, legal testimony has various rhetorical advantages for the speech act approach adopted by Coady. In order to define something as a speech act, the conditions by which we can recognize that act must be established. For example, the phrase "I do" only completes the speech act of getting married if it is uttered at the proper place in a wedding ceremony, by one of the parties getting married, supervised by a properly authorized official. The model of legal testimony gives Coady an explicit set of conditions from which he can derive a definition for all forms of testimony. In the legal setting, the qualifications of the witness and the conditions under which she may testify are explicitly defined. On television, testimonial video had to be recognized by the viewer without necessarily being marked as such by the immediate context in which it airs.

From the rules for legal testimony, Coady derives three conditions for a statement to qualify as natural testimony:

> A speaker S testifies by making statement p if and only if:
> 1. His stating that p is evidence that p and p is offered as evidence that p.
> 2. S has the relevant competence, authority or credentials to state truly that p.
> 3. S's statement is relevant to some disputed or unresolved question (which may or may not be p) and is directed to those who are in need of evidence on the matter. (42)

As Coady points out, courts use protocols to ensure that any testimony entered into evidence meets these three conditions. Legal testimony meets the first condition, since courts classify testimony as evidence, only allowing it to appear in the evidentiary phase of the trial, rather than in the opening and closing statements; furthermore, the witness must identify his statements as testimony by taking an oath. The second condition about the competence of the witness is met by the rules about who can testify and the oath administered to each witness. Like all other evidence presented in court, testimony must be relevant to matters at issue in the case or it will be excluded.

According to Coady's three-point definition, we can understand Holiday's tape as testimony on television and as evidence in court. On television, the tape was offered as public evidence of the beating. The unusual formal qualities of the image marked it as authentic testimony, captured with nonprofessional equipment while the incident was unfolding. The outrage about the beating shows that the audience needed to see the image to become aware of police behavior.

In court, the arguments made by either side determine what evidence will be relevant to the case. In the case of testimonial video on television, something can call for proof because the audience does not believe it or attend to it. The Holidays felt that the tape had to be shown because such beatings were not supposed to happen in the United States. Having emigrated from Argentina, they associated such state violence with their old country. In the case of videos depicting traumatic events, the need for evidence takes on a particular affective force. In order to open a dialogue with the authorities and inquire into what happened, proof was needed. Coady defines testimony as a speech act, but Holiday's tape involves at least two kinds of locution: testimony and the demand for justice. It was offered as both proof that something had happened and a means for finding out why it had occurred.

Coady only considers testimony in the form of speech and writing. Today, many additional testimonial media have emerged. Whether or not testimonial images can be conceived of by Coady's speech act theory based method, we have seen an influential appeals court decision refer to certain evidentiary films as "pictorial representation of witness testimony."[5]

While the modern public sphere was virtually produced by the transformation of moveable type, the contemporary public sphere is produced by the transmission of moving images. The equipment needed to produce, disseminate, and review moving images has been incorporated into the infrastructures of our institutions, and moving images have become a standard means by which the business of our institutions is accomplished. The electronic public sphere provides the key context for testimonial video. Among other things, Coady's omission occludes the possibility that something may be presented as testimony in one context, but not in another, which is precisely what happened to Holiday's tape. Screened on international television, the tape functioned as mechanical, visual testimony corroborating the story told by the anchor. Its contents were never questioned. As we have seen, in courts, motion pictures function altogether differently.

Holiday's tape presented the occasion for the emergence of the phrase "testimonial video" outside the courts. On television, testimonial video might be thought of as a special case of what Coady calls "natural testimony." Perhaps the best description of the contextual factors allowing us to recognize a tape as testimonial on television comes from one of the essays that first worked with the concept of "testimonial video," Avital Ronell's "Trauma TV: 12 Steps Beyond the Pleasure Principle," a difficult, suggestive, and moving essay. According to the piece, Holiday's tape testifies both to the specific occurrence that it documents and to a quotidian, domestic violence, which usually takes place out of frame, obscured by the shadows of plausible deniability. Ronell's analysis shows that the tape was able to testify on television because of the formal contrast between it and other programming.

Holiday's tape was dark, illuminated only by streetlights and headlights. Holiday shot it at a considerable distance from the action, using only his zoom lens and slight pans and tilts to control the framing. The texture of the tape is grainy and the bodies on it appear slightly indistinct. All of these formal features violate the masterful and lucid norms of television production. They set the tape off in such a way that the audience sees it as a report of something, a report made under duress for the purpose of testifying to what it shows.

Ronell's piece acknowledges that not every image with such features is testimonial—some are meant to silence the reality of what they show. She argues that Holiday's tape took the place of the unconscious of the sanitized televisual images of the first Gulf War. The Holiday tape and the images of Baghdad being bombed have the same look, the same visual texture, but the images of the first Gulf War hide the violence of the bombing while the King tape exposes violence on the domestic front. The visual similarities between the two images allows Ronell to see them as completing one another, and surely her reading has something in common with the public's reaction to the King tape, which was broadcast in the context of the war. Such considerations, however, had no relevance to the trial.

Ronell distinguishes between testimonial video and ordinary television journalism. The differential relationship between these two image modalities is encrypted in the "TV" of her title, which stands for both "television" and "testimonial video." For Ronell, testimonial video is "at once outside and inside TV" (311), in the sense that although testimonial video appears on television, it is made according to different protocols. Testimonial video must be shown on a television to be seen at all since its testimonial power derives from its difference with that context, from the fact that it does not obey the semantic and syntactic rules that govern normal and normative television productions.

Ronell opens up questions about a possible ethics of the tele-spectator within by exploring these differences. Holiday's tape gives rise to an ethics of the tele-spectator by showing the violence repressed in other images on television and which the spectator tends to ignore or to repress. It transmits what the viewer cannot easily resolve, which needs to be watched again and again. For Ronell, these differences mark testimonial video as a report of a trauma.

Like oral testimony to trauma, film and video testimony about trauma of the type discussed by Ronell differs from ordinary testimony and those differences take the form of failures or limits. It bears symptoms on its visual surface. Deviations from the norms of speech mark the trauma survivor's testimony and differences from the institutional norms of video production mark testimonial videos depicting trauma. In both cases the variations from the norm take the form of limitations or incapacities. Well-known symptoms in video and film testimony to trauma include the dark spectrality of the tape of King's beating, the enforced distance countervailing the drive to see in the tapes of the World Trade Center burning in 2001, the images' haziness in the Waco, Texas, conflagration, and the haphazard framing in Allied troops' films of Auschwitz. The imperfections of all those images correspond to the stutter, the silence, the mortified or hyperemotional tone in oral testimony. They are each a disruption of the codes of recording and representation. They are the result of a historical circumstance frustrating the scopic drive; they are gashes cut into the image by the very conditions of

the trauma to which they testify. In each case there were few if any other
ways that the images could have been shot and the situations did not
allow time to plan the recording. The structure and symptomology of oral testimony to trauma has
been extensively elucidated by psychoanalysts. While many of psycho-
analytic conclusions pertain only to spoken testimony, this general
model helps to account for the tape's ability to function as testimony on
television in a way in which it could not in court.

According to the psychoanalytic model, listening to, receiving testimony to trauma, differs from ordinary listening insofar as to be
understandable, such testimony needs to be brought into a symbolic
order by the listener, since the trauma causes its survivor to lose their
relation to meaning. The force of trauma collapses the overarching
framework of meaning that would otherwise make sense of what happened and allow it to be understood as an experience. Moreover, listening to testimony to trauma affects the receiver's relation to the
symbolic, as if the trauma were infectious.

In their book *Testimony: The Crisis of Witnessing in Literature,
Psychoanalysis and History*, Shoshana Felman and Dori Laub define the
role of the listener. Felman and Laub write that the one who listens to
testimony about a trauma is "the blank screen on which the event comes
to be inscribed as experience for the first time" (Felman and Laub) (57).
The speaker's trauma has so alienated him from meaning that he has not
been able to register it as experience, that is, as an event understandable
within the symbolic order. Like Coady's definition of ordinary testimony,
Felman and Laub's description of testimony to trauma casts testimony as
a speech act, but for them the listener must complete the act in order for
it to be successful. The role of the listener is implicit in Coady's stipu-
lation that testimony must refer to something that needs proving. Who is
in need of such evidence if not the listener? But for Felman and Laub
testimony involves an attempt at the restitution of a broken symbolic order
through the act of listening and, since the witness has not yet experienced
his own trauma, he needs the testimony as well. In other words, the
listener makes it possible for the witness to mean anything at all, by
allowing the witness to connect the experiencing self he has become
since the trauma with the experiencing self he was before it, suturing over
the existential wound he bears. The listener becomes a screen, a surface
that makes it possible to inscribe the trauma as an experience. Only when

it is inscribed does the trauma become legible, not only for the receiver, but for the witness.

The testifier's very survival is bound up with this resistance to experiencing a trauma that has no spatial or temporal limits. This resistance to giving and receiving testimony, to having our cognition overwhelmed by the account, partly motivated the compulsive, repeated screenings of such tapes.

When someone testifies to a trauma that they have undergone or witnessed, they are, according to Felman and Laub, giving form to a moment that had overwhelmed them and impaired their capacity to observe and remember. The moment of massive trauma does not take the form of an experience until it is told and listened to. In an experience or an event the subject comes into contact with something, even if that thing is none other than the subject itself. In a trauma, Felman and Laub suggest, the wounded psyche folds itself into an abyss in which it seeks shelter from the real and symbolic blows that rupture its protective skin. Such a retreat into an abyss causes the subject to temporarily vanish and only in the *ex post facto* telling does the subject meet the trauma as experience, since before the testimony the trauma is not experienced because the subject had been absent at the traumatic moment.

Felman and Laub show that the listener provides a screen on which meaning can be produced from the trauma. Their image of the listener as screen suggests that she provides a frame that gives the trauma a context and provides a modicum of protection to the teller. The listener as screen provides context within which the trauma can be made to signify, as well as a certain distance between the traumatic real and the teller. These are two aspects of the same function. Before being projected on such a screen a trauma does not have any meaning. The traumatism of trauma defies the symbolic so that the trauma remains uncoded, unutterable, and invisible. Assimilating the trauma into the symbolic order by telling it holds the real at bay by reducing its raw force to the signifying structures of experience.

Felman and Laub's image of the listener as screen echoes in the aural register the screen that Jacques Lacan inserts into the increasingly famous conical diagram of the gaze that he presents in *The Four Fundamental Concepts of Psychoanalysis*. Lacan's screen has been interpreted as the cultural reserve of images that give every individual image the possibility of meaning,[6] by which we map ourselves into the visual field. The screen is of the symbolic order—it produces meaning and allows the subject to take its place.

Within the screen, forms that accommodate scopophilia are the norm. Images that exhibit mastery over the objects represented serve the scopic drive. The fantasy of being a full subject, with the represented object both utterly available and held at a safe remove, is induced by scenes that can be presented from the most aesthetically pleasing angle, that can be shown to maximize the quantity of information given by the image. In such images, seeing lords over the represented, and so they exhibit the quality of mastery.

Testimonial film and video cannot accommodate masterful vision. Fragments of the real are lodged in the wounds borne by such images, fragments that cannot be reduced to signifying elements and so puncture the screen like shrapnel. In making the trauma into an event through its telling, both the teller and the listener are committed to getting it right. Yet at the same time both teller and listener resist the pressure of the trauma. Often the listener fails in the attempt to provide a symbolic order in which the trauma can make sense. The listener resists and defends against the telling of trauma. When we hear such testimony we become numb, angry at the teller, flooded with overblown sentiment, or so obsessed with the facts of the trauma that we neglect the testifier (72–73). As Felman writes, "testimony is composed of events that overwhelm our sense of cognition," so we put up our defenses in order to keep our frame of reference (5). We do not want to hear and remember what we have heard for fear that we will absorb the trauma and it will tear us apart. We do not want to take the place of the screen for the teller out of fear that the testimony will puncture us.

Because of this resistance, because testimony of this kind is the creation of experience from shock, it is marked by symptoms both in the teller and the listener. Experience does not emerge from the abyss smoothly; shock is not transparently converted into knowledge. Testimony about trauma, Felman and Laub point out, is marked by silences, stammerings, numb monotone, and tears. These symptoms are the traces of the damage done to the testifier's sense of the symbolic order. They constitute a resistance to testifying and to the new trauma that is inflicted at the moment when such a discourse is produced, whether it takes the form of speech or image.

Tele-Pathy

Scopophilia is the drive that forces us to attempt to see the unseen remainder of images. When the exigencies of the real derail the pleasure of a masterful view of an event, a strong affect is produced: the drive cannot satisfy itself against the screen of mastery. The gashes in the screen repulse the drive until it overflows and produces our discomfort at such images.

The Los Angeles courts allowed a change of venue on the trial of the police officers who beat King because of the strong affect produced by the broadcast of Holiday's tape. The decision to move the trial of the officers who beat him from Los Angeles to Simi Valley, a conservative Southern California community with a large population of retired police, was based on the wide dissemination of the tape and the response that it received. In that decision, Judges Klein, Danielson, Croskey, and Heinz of California's Second District Court of Appeals use a prophetic figure of speech when they wrote that after the tape was broadcast "a firestorm immediately developed in the Los Angeles area, so intense and pervasive was the reaction to the videotape" (*Powell v. Superior Court*). They explain that their decision to move the trial away from Los Angeles is based on more than the extensive extralegal exhibition of the tape:

> We emphasize... that were this simply a matter of extraordinary publicity we might have reached a different conclusion. What compels our decision in this case is the high level of political turmoil and controversy that the incident has generated. (779)

The jurists wrote that "from its initial showing, the predictable reaction ranged from shock, outrage, revulsion and fear to disbelief—all powerful human emotions to be capitalized on by the media" (780). Testimonial motion pictures transmit traumatic affect from their wounds to ours, transmitting from symptom to symptom. Imperfection and incommensurability are the relays of a silent, haunting scream. Following Jacques Derrida's usage of the prefix "tele-" in *The Post Card*, we might call this form of broadcasting tele-pathy—feeling at a distance.

In Lacan's description of the scopic field, seeing is done by a subject within the same space as that which she sees. Once the camera is taken into consideration, a temporal element must be added to this structure. The temporality of evidentiary film and video is not the time of the take that generates cinema's unique relation to duration, but the temporality of the distribution, screening, and rescreening of the image. An image produced by a camera can in principle always be shown at another place and another time. This structural possibility is the "tele" of television.

Video testimony as tele-pathy is a manifestation of the compound effects of difference and deferral introduced into the visual field by the camera. The images of the traumatic can only perform their public function and can only transmit their affect, because those images are seen in a different space from where they occurred and at a time deferred from the moment of occurrence. That *différance* makes the image iterable. It allows the qualities of the look to work outside of meaning even while the so-called "content" of the image is integrated into the symbolic register. In the tele-pathy of the testimonial image, we are opened to the trauma of the other when the traumatized Other in ourselves is awakened. The distance of the "tele" only brings us back to a repressed segment of ourselves. What is at stake here is a certain transference whereby memories of our own wounds play upon the image that flickers in front of us. Those memories do not constitute a screen but rather the unhealed ruptures of our own look. When we see an image of trauma with its unmastered form we feel our own vision as traumatized. Though we resist and attempt to see more—to see what the image does not show—we fail and so we take on the other's wounded optic in the form of our own traumatized gaze.

Tele-pathy is the defining remainder of the testimonial moving image. It is the structure in the film and video testimony that resists any institutionalization. The courts turned away from the limitations of Holiday's tape and the affect these limitations produced. For the legal institution, the tape provided access to the facts of Rodney King's beating. The limitations in that image, however, are precisely that which made it testimonial and were the source of the cultural compulsion to repeat the image across a number of institutions. Testimonial moving images are repeated because they fail to find a proper screen—a context within which they can become meaningful and fully visible by virtue of being articulated within the symbolic order. Holiday's tape spread beyond the news media and the courts. It remained a *hors d'oeuvre* in Spike Lee's *Malcolm X*. It does not fit in the Whitney Biennial.

Screening Out the Tele-Path

The limitations of Holiday's tape could not be seen as marks of trauma when the tape was shown in court. In the context of commercial television productions, the formal characteristics of the tape appeared as wounds inflicted on the image by the trauma it recorded. Those wounds served as guarantors of the tape's authenticity and activated its telepathic, testimonial power. The tape appeared as testimony because it was surrounded by other images whose mastery gave its limitations their value. At trial, the tape was not seen as an image surrounded by other images but as an image within an argument. The tape's authenticity was not guaranteed by any of its formal qualities but by Holiday's testimony. Ronell's argument constitutes testimonial video within the frame of commercial television. It is because she does not note the particularity of the frame that she is surprised by the court's failure, in another framework, to hear that testimony.

Commercial television frames brutality as something visible. Fiction and nonfiction programs have developed an iconography of violence, and an iconography of race, in the context of which institutionalized racist violence appears as visible. In court, police brutality is not something that can simply be seen. Certain types of blows and certain ways of restraining a suspect are against the law. However, the determination of police brutality as such requires a judgment that goes beyond the immediacy of seeing. To decide if police have used excessive force, jurors must compare what officers did in a given case with what they were trained to do—jurors must decide whether police acted as a "reasonable officer" would have. Such judgments cannot be made only by looking at an image.

The force of the Holiday tape's testimonial appearance on television, outside the courtroom, led the prosecution to assume that the tape would speak for itself in court. Their case relied on the tape alone to convince the jury that the police had used excessive force. The prosecution was blind to the changing value of the tape and assumed that its testimonial aspect would be as visible in court as it was on television. When the defense presented the tape as part of their case, they used a variety of analytic techniques to break the tape's testimonial effect. On television the tape seemed to show one thing. By showing sections of the tape as a series of stills printed on cards as well as freeze-framed on a monitor, for example, the defense was able to open up the possibility that the tape showed the opposite of what it seemed to show, Rodney King attacking the police officers. On television, the tape was initially shown with little commentary or with Holiday's narration of what he saw. The defense took these measures to ensure that the tape became physical evidence to be analyzed technically, rather than testimony affectively proving what it showed.

The defense also took tactical advantage of the out of frame, claiming that Rodney King's behavior before the camera started shooting motivated his beating. However, the tape's testimony was muted in court precisely because it was offered as an index of King's beating. Holiday's serendipitously recorded tape was offered as a showing without a seeing subject. The tape was able to function as proof that the beating occurred only insofar as it appeared without implying a point of view, allowing those present in court to see the beating for themselves. By changing the tape from testimony to a nonsubjective seeing, the defense was able to diminish the tape's power. The marks of trauma on the image are not readable as such on a nonsubjective seeing. Those marks produce the effects of testimonial tele-pathy only by virtue of a relation with the sight of a presumed subject—a masterful subject that provides the model of all subjectivity. Any presumption of the other's optic would prevent the image from appearing as nonsubjective and the marks of trauma, the surface of the image, becomes invisible, leaving only competing accounts of what it shows. The nonsubjective vision is immediately reduced from optical material to a set of facts, but the wounded sight of testimonial video is precisely a matter of its optical materiality.

The materiality of vision disappears in the process of translating the image into a set of facts. In *People v. Powel et al.* the defense controlled the translation of Holiday's tape into facts through the use of expert testimony. They also presented the tape in a variety of ways, controlling the speed of the tape, freezing the image at select moments, and applying transparencies of still photographs to the screen.[7] Because the prosecution offered the tape to prove something that was not entirely visible (e.g., the use of excessive force), the defense was able to solicit testimony that the image suggested something else.

Courts accepted videotape as proof of what it showed, if what it showed was strictly speaking visible. In one of the Abscam trails, *United States v. Weisz* (1983), videotape was used to show that a United States congressman accepted a bribe. Although bribery is not, strictly speaking, a visible act, that tape had a soundtrack so that the transaction could be heard, and every step of the narrative was filmed, from the offer to the taking of the money. The government was at great pains to make sure that the congressman could be seen taking the money. The tape let the offer be heard and let all the visible components be seen.

Although Holiday's tape showed the police brutally beating King, the question of police brutality can only be answered through a comparison. As nonsubjective seeing, the tape was only an index of the physical positions of those involved in the event. The defense took advantage of the necessity for comparison in order to solicit expert testimony that construed the tape as an image of reasonable police procedure. Witnesses testified that King appeared to be charging the officers in certain frames of the tape. The courts framed the tape's testimony to trauma so that its tele-pathic aspect was completely screened out.

The prosecuting attorneys assumed that Holiday's video would prove police misconduct in court, just as it has on television. The naturalization and valorization of evidentiary video over the previous two decades left the prosecutors unprepared for the defense's reading of the evidence. The unexpected conflict between the way the tape played on television and the way it played in court initiated a new phase in the history of evidentiary motion pictures. The assimilation of film and video into the courts was complete. Moving images had sat atop a hierarchy of evidence, but that hierarchy fell apart. When the Holiday tape was shown in advance of the trial, the public took it as the truth, the key piece of evidence, seen by all. But the trial left evidentiary video as one among many forms of recorded evidence, none of them particularly privileged. The shift was marked by a city in flames.

Between the late 1910s and the early 1990s, U.S. courts assimilated motion pictures, creating a mutable category, "motion picture evidence," through which to conceptualize them. Lawyers discovered they could admit films into evidence by laying the proper testimonial foundation. The more elaborate the foundation, the more probative it became, until, finally, with enough testimony a film could trump an eyewitness account. By the era of video evidence, motion pictures required little foundation-building. They were taken to be the most reliable form of evidence, the top of the hierarchy. The King case collapsed the hierarchy, and with that collapse a phase of motion picture history also came to an end.

We could refer to that process as the integration of moving images into the legal system, or we could call it deconstruction. This book describes the imposition onto a hierarchy of what it once excluded, the domination of the hierarchy by the formerly excluded term, and a resultant dissolution of the hierarchy. Here, deconstruction takes an intuitional form, at first multiplying the forms of codification the juridical institution used to handle evidence and then giving wider and wider scope to improvisation. In our context the rise of improvisation amounts to the legal system institutionalizing a form of lawlessness in an attempt to incorporate what had been a foreign technology. The technology is now firmly entrenched.

Notes

Chapter 1

1. An example of such usage can be found on page 68 of David Bordwell and Kristin Thompson's textbook *Film Art*. "In everyday life, we perceive things around us in a practical way. But in a film the things that happen to be on screen serve no practical end for us." These sentences come from a passage about formal expectations in cinematic films, and sound highly plausible in that context. Evidentiary film clearly shows the jury objects of practical importance insofar as they must decide the facts of a case; however, as Christian Metz pointed out, without a modifier, "film" means cinema (*Metz*) (45).

2. While not much attention has been paid to the specificity of other institutions, scholars have addressed the specificity of cinematic institutions. See, for example, David Bordwell, Janet Staiger, and Kristin Thompson, *The Classical Hollywood Cinema: Film Style & Mode of Production to 1960* (New York: Columbia University Press, 1985).

3. For a recent study of "medium specificity" in film theory and the problems attending it see D. N. Rodwick, *The Virtual Life Of Film* (Cambridge, Mass.: Harvard University Press, 2007).

4. See for example, Paolo Cherchi Usai, *The Death of Cinema: History, Cultural Memory, and the Digital Dark Age* (London: The British Film Institute, 2001).

5. The crudeness of many film theorists' notion of indexicality and their willingness to see it where it may not be has been argued by Philip Rosen in "History of Image: Image of History: Subject and Ontology in Bazin" in *Rites of Realism: Essays on Corporeal Cinema*, ed. Ivone Margulies (Durham, N.C.: Duke University Press, 2003).

Chapter 3

1. The *American Law Review* note cited above summarizes past practice as a guide for lawyers and judges. However there can be a lag between the case law culled in such

notes and juridical practices contemporaneous with their publication. In this case, the note does not account for the new, shorter form of authentication.

2. The first note on motion pictures as evidence appears in the 1933 volume of *American Law Reports Annotated*. In this note, only one of the cases cited involves films offered to prove malingering. The next note on motion pictures as evidence, published in 1940, cites five cases involving films offered to show that the plaintiff had exaggerated claims of disability. Neither of these two notes name this kind of film among the classes of motion picture evidence. The following *American Law Reports Annotated* note on motion picture evidence classifies such films as films used "to show malingering or physical condition of party" (Rogers) (698). This note from the 1958 volume of *American Law Reports Annotated*, second series, cites no less than sixteen cases in this section, to which it devotes four pages.

3. Films offered into evidence to show malingering represent a logical development of medical images in the juridical sphere. X-rays and photographs of injuries accompanied by the testimony of a physician had been presented as evidence before the use of films showing supposedly injured subjects acting in ways that should be prevented by their injuries. Evidentiary medical images conjoined the framing of a scientific discipline with that of the courts. The medical framing of images is elaborated in Lisa Cartwright's germinal study *Screening the Body*. She shows that medical films impose an analytic gaze on the body, subjecting the soma's messy fluid processes to organization and quantification. This gaze permits the establishment of a set of norms, that disguise the social components of certain biological categories such as race and gender. The power effects produced by those categories are occluded by the medical framing of images that makes the physician's gaze appear to be the fundamental form of perception from which scientific facts are derived.

Whereas the social effects of medical films occur under the cover of the discipline's supposed neutrality, malingering films are blatantly instrumentalized. Although malingering films are framed so as to be free of any particular gaze, and presented as incontrovertible indices of physical facts, they are not made to determine the truth of a claimant's condition. They are made to convince the jury that the claimant does not have a condition. They are created to persuade rather than to find a truth. To accomplish that goal, malingering films must be presented as objective, despite the fact that they are part of an argument. While medical films mold a certain truth, malingering films are suasional. Medical films are only intelligible to those with specialized knowledge. If they are to persuade a jury they must be explained as well as authenticated. Malingering films are made so that the jury can understand what they show without any expert testimony, and they are often used against the expert testimony of physicians.

The structure of the trial in the adversarial legal system is such that testimony or physical evidence is not often presented by one of the parties in litigation merely because it is true. Testimony and evidence are presented because they support the argument of the side making the presentation. The rhetoric of making a case at trial thus gives all evidence and testimony presented in court a blatantly instrumental character. As we have seen, this is most obvious in cases in which the films offered are suspect. In the Harris and Williamson cases, the cross-examination of the witness who authenticated the films destroyed that witness's credibility and that of the films. The films offered in those cases are clearly attempts to use the effect of objectivity produced by motion pictures to persuade the jury. The same can be said of the highlight reel presented in *DeBattiste v. Anthony Laudadio & Son.*

Chapter 4

1. The rules set out in the guidelines are not laws. However, lawyers could argue for the admission of a videotaped deposition on the grounds that its form met all the standards set out by the Federal Justice Center, and such an argument carried weight with judges.

2. The names of the parties involved in the stimulus case were anglicized in order to eliminate race as a factor in the experiment (Miller, 1979).

3. See Ferdinand de Saussure, *Course in General Linguistics* (New York: McGraw-Hill Book Company, 1959), pp. 107–111.

4. This headline shows an assumption about the functional equivalence of film and video in the general discourse of the public sphere as well in the discourse of jurists.

5. This connection is more than a humorous aside. It is an important part of the frame in which motion pictures appear in court. Miller and Fontes write that they were "convinced that juror expectations concerning trial process are significantly shaped by courtroom drama presented on television" (Miller, 1979).

6. The one interesting series of articles in the *New York Times* on evidentiary motion pictures between 1974 and 1978 concerns President Gerald Ford's court-ordered videotaped deposition in the trial of Lynette "Squeaky" Fromme in 1975. He was the first president to testify in a criminal trial while in office, and the fact that he did so on tape only furthered the acceptance of video in the courts by showing that it made possible the testimony of such a prestigious, busy man.

7. Hemphill's opinion helped set a federal precedent and was cited in several federal appeals opinions from this period (e.g., *Field v. Omaha Standard; Durflinger v. Artiles*).

8. A motion in *limine* is a motion held just before the start of trial, usually concerning evidentiary issues.

9. The rule reads, "Although relevant, evidence may be excluded if its probative value is substantially outweighed by the danger of unfair prejudice, confusion of the issues, or misleading the jury, or considerations of undue delay, waste of time, or needless presentation of cumulative evidence" (*Federal Rules of Evidence*) (27).

10. The court's framing of video as a window onto the facts was supported by yet another use of motion picture evidence and the history of precedent that allowed it. One of the earliest uses of films and photographs in court was to present an experiment that could not conveniently be performed at trial. In the 1970s and 1980s the use of taped experiments increased dramatically as litigation over complex technology skyrocketed and the production of moving images in the scientific community multiplied. The admissibility of such tapes is determined chiefly by the admissibility of the experiments that they depict. If the experiment bears a substantial similarity to the events before the court, or if it illustrates the testimony of an expert witness, the tape is admissible. Case law assumes that the medium of video is completely transparent in such tapes. The assumption of transparency is a common factor in many heterogeneous uses of film and video, and the dissemination of that assumption works to render the class of evidentiary motion pictures as a whole emphatically indexical. Cases that deal with videos of experiments in this period include *Slakan v. Porter et al., Brewer v. Jeep Corporation,* and *Conti v. Ford Motor Co.*

11. The out of frame and the invisible haunt the moving image. They can be used to argue that an image is of something that it only suggests, as in this case, and, as Jim Lastra has pointed out in the last chapter of his dissertation, the out of frame can always be used to vitiate the truth effects of an image (Lastra, 1992). This also occurred in the first trial of the police officers who beat Rodney King.

12. It is important to remember that the distinction between form and content is part of the juridical framing of the motion picture and not an inherent feature of the moving image. The use of this distinction allowed judges to see film as a window through which the court could see facts. The problem of discerning the difference between objective signifiers and signifiers of objectivity, delineated in the section on the Federal Justice Center's *Guidelines For Pre-Recording Testimony on Videotape Prior to Trial*, applies to the use of the categories of form and content by judges as well.

13. Lawyers usually provide an argument in the face of contingency. Attorneys will make contradictory arguments to the court if they feel that any such argument might advance their case. Arguments that fail fall by the wayside.

14. The foundational witness of a video is the person who testifies as to the authenticity of the tape. Often that witness is asked a series of questions about the tape in order to guide the jury's attention to certain facts it depicts, and this depiction is then to be considered in drawing inferences about the facts in the case.

15. See, for example, James L. McCrystal and Ann B. Maschari, "PRVTT: A Lifeline for the Jury System" in *Trial* (March 1983).

16. The rule reads, "the contents of voluminous writings, recordings, or photographs which cannot conveniently be examined in court may be presented by a chart, summary, or calculation. The originals or duplicates shall be made available for examination or copying or both by other parties at a reasonable time and place. The court may order that they be produced in court" (*Federal Rules of Evidence*) (481).

Chapter 5

1. For an elucidation of the concept of an image-event, see Retort's *Afflicted Powers: Capital and Spectacle in a New Age of War* (Verso, 2005).

2. See Stan Chanbers, http://www.citivu.com/ktla/sc-ch1b.html.

3. See http://www.guardian.co.uk/fromthearchive/story/0,,1009004,00.html.

4. This difference between the video and testimony, the courts need for authenticating testimony, was noted by Jacques Derrida in *Echographies: Of Television*.

5. As stated in *International Union, United Automobile, Aircraft and Agricultural Implement Workers of America, C. I. O. et al. v. Paul S. Russell*.

6. See, for example, Hal Foster's essay "Obscene, Abject, Traumatic" in *October* 78.

7. See http://query.nytimes.com/gst/fullpage.html?res=9E0CE3DE173FF932A25750 C0A9649582́60.

Bibliography

A. L. Harmon v. San Joaquin Light & Power Corporation. *Reports of Cases Determined in the District Courts of Appeal of the State of California.* San Francisco: Bancroft-Whitney, 1940. 169–175. Vol. 37.

Andelman, David A. "Videotape to Be Used in Bronx in U.S. Pilot Program." *New York Times* December 9, 1974: 29.

Andrew, Dudley. *André Bazin.* New York: Columbia University Press, 1978.

Arnheim, Rudolf. *Film As Art.* Berkeley. Univeristy of California Press.

Associated Press. "Videotape Trial Held in Vermont." *New York Times* June 23 1973: 32.

Aumont, Jacques, et al. *Aesthetics of Film.* Trans. Richard Neopert. Austin: University of Texas Press, 1983.

Bazin, André. "Ontologie de l'image photgraphique." *Qu'est-ce que le cinema.* Ed. André Bazin. Paris: Les Édition Du Cerf, 1990. 9–17.

——. "The Ontology of the Photographic Image." *What Is Cinema?* Trans. Hugh Gray. Berkeley: University of California, 1967. Vol. 1.

——. "Theater and Cinema." *What Is Cinema.* Ed. Hugh Grey. Trans. Hugh Grey. Berkeley: University of California Press, 1967. Vol. 1.

Borch-Jacobsen, Mikkel. *Lacan: The Absolute Master.* Trans. Douglas Brick. Stanford, Calif.: Stanford University Press, 1991.

Bordwell, David, and Kristin Thompson. *Film Art.* Fifth Edition ed. New York: McGraw-Hill, 1997.

Bordwell, David; Janet Staiger, and Kristin Thompson. *The Classical Hollywood Cinema: Film Style & Mode of Production to 1960,* by New York. Columbia University Press, 1985.

Boyarsky v. G. A. Zimmerman Corporation et al. *New York Supplement.* St Paul: West Publishing. 1934. 134–241.

Brunette, Peter, and David Wills. "The Spatial Arts: An Interview With Jacques Derrida."
    Deconstruction and the Visual Arts: Art, Media, Architecture. Eds. Peter Brunette
    and David Wills. Cambridge: Cambridge University Press, 1994. 9–33.
Butler, Judith. "Endangered, Endangering: Schematic Racism and White Paranoia."
    Reading Rodney King, Reading Urban Uprising. Ed. Robert Gooding-Williams.
    New York: Routledge, 1993.
Cartwright, Lisa. *Screening The Body.* Minneapolis: University of Minnesota Press, 1995.
Coady, C. A. J. *Testimony: A Philosophical Study.* Oxford: Oxford University Press, 1992.
Commonwealth v. Harold Roller. Pennsylvania Superior Court Reports. Harrisburg: The
    Telegraph, 1931. 125–131. Vol. 100.
Conley, Tom. *Film Hieroglyphics: Ruptures in Classical Cinema.* Minneapolis: University
    of Minnesota Press, 1991.
DeBattiste v. Anthony Laudadio & Son et al. Pennsylvania Superior Court Reports. Sayre,
    Pa.: Murrelle, 1950. 38–44. Vol. 167.
DeCamp v. United States. Federal Reporter. St. Paul: West Publishing, 1926. Vol. 10.
DeGuy, Michel, ed. *Au Sujet de Shoah: le film de Claude Lanzmann.* Paris: Belin, 1990.
Deleuze, Gilles. *Cinema 1: The Movement Image.* Trans. Hugh Tomlinson and Barbara
    Habberjam. Minneapolis: University of Minnesota Press, 1986.
Derrida, Jacques. *The Post Card: From Socrates to Freud and Beyond.* Trans. Allan Bass.
    Chicago: University of Chicago Press, 1987.
———. *The Truth In Painting.* Trans. Geoff Bennington and Ian McLeod. Chicago:
    University of Chicago Press, 1987.
———. *La Vérité En Peinture.* Paris: Flammarion, 1978.
———. *Writing and Difference.* Trans. Alan Bass. Chicago: University of Chicago Press,
    1978.
———. *Of Grammatology.* Trans. Gayatri Spivak. Baltimore: Johns Hopkins University
    Press, 1974.
Federal Rules of Evidence For United States Courts and Magistrates. St. Paul: West
    Publishing, 1992.
Feeny v. Young. The New York Supplement. St. Paul: West Publishing, 1920. Vol. 181.
Felman, Shoshana, and Dori Laub. *Testimony: The Crisis of Witnessing in Literature,
    Psychoanalysis, and History.* New York: Routledge, 1992.
Foster, Hal. "Obscene, Abject, Traumatic." *October* 78 (1996). 107–124.
Friedman, Lawrence. *Crime And Punishment in American History.* New York: Basic
    Books, 1993.
Gibson v. Gunn. The New York Supplement with Key Number Annotations. St. Paul: West
    Publishing, 1923. Vol. 202.
Gooding-Williams, Robert, ed. *Reading Rodney King/Reading Urban Uprising.* New York:
    Routledge, 1993.
Guidelines For Pre-Recording Testimony on Videotape Prior to Trial. Washington: The
    Federal Judicial Center, 1976.
*Gulf Research Development Co. v. Linder. Cases Argued and Decided in the Supreme
    Court of Mississippi.* Colombia, Mo.: E. W. Stephens, 1936. 123–134. Vol. 177.
Harris v. St. Louis Public Service Company. South Western Reporter Second Series.
    St. Paul: West Publishing, 1954. 850–857. Vol. 270.

Heiman et al. v. Market St. Railroad. Co. Pacific Court Reports 2nd Series. St. Paul Minn.: West Publishing, 1937. 179–181. Vol. 69.

Heller, Fred I., ed. Advanced Litigation Skills Using Video. New York: Practicing Law Institute, 1987.

———. Video Techniques in Trial and Pretrial. New York: Practicing Law Institute, 1983.

International Union, United Automobile, Aircraft and Agricultural Implement Workers of America, C. I. O. et al. v. Paul S. Russell, Report of Cases Argued and Determined in the Supreme Court of Alabama. St. Paul: West Publishing, 1956. 456–473. Vol. 264.

Joseph, Gregory P. Modern Visual Evidence. New York: Law Journal Seminars-Press, 1990.

———. "Demonstrative Videotape Evidence." Trial June 1986.

"Judge at Murder Trial Bars Films Depicting Story of the Defendant." The Moving Picture World, February 21, 1920: 1257.

Kennedy, Herbert H. "Motion Pictures in Evidence." Illinois Law Review 27: 424–427. 1933.

Lacan, Jacques. Le Séminaire de Jacques Lacan livre XVII: L'Envers de la psychanalyse, 1969–70. Eds. Jacques-Alain Miller and Judith Miller. Paris: Éditions du Seuil, 1991.

———. The Four Fundamental Concepts of Psychoanalysis. Trans. Alan Sheridan. New York: Norton, 1973.

LaCapra, Dominick. "Lanzmann's Shoah: 'Here There Is No Why.' Critical Inquiry 23.2 (1997): 231–269.

Lanzmann, Claude. "Seminar With Claude Lanzmann, 11 April 1990." Yale French Studies 79 (1991): 82–99.

———. "Le Lieu et La Parole." Au Sujet de Shoah: le film de Claude Lanzmann. Paris: Belin, 1990.

———. Shoah. Paris: Fayard, 1985.

Laplanche, J., and J. B. Pontalis. The Language of Psychoanalysis. Trans. Donald Nicholson-Smith. New York: W. W. Norton & Company, 1973.

Lastra, James. "Standards And Practices: Technology and Representation in the American Cinema." Ph.D. Dissertation. University of Iowa, 1992.

"Law School Opens Model Courtroom." New York Times. October 7, 1973: 76.

Levinas, Emmanuel. Existence and Existents. Trans. Alphonso Lingus. Dordrecht: Kluwer Academic Publishers, 1978.

Lindsay, Vachel. The Art Of The Moving Picture. New York: Macmillan Co., 1915.

MacEvoy, J. P. "Tricked into Acting." Reader's Digest. February, 1940. pp. 70–73.

Mary B. Williamson v. St Louis Public Service Company. Reports of Cases Determined by the Supreme Court of the State of Missouri. Columbia, Mo.: E. W. Stephens, 1952. 508–521. Vol. 363.

Maryland Casualty Company v. Coker. Federal Reporter Second Series. St. Paul: West Publishing, 1941. 43–44. Vol. 118.

Massachusetts Bonding & Ins. Co. v. Worthy. South Western Reports Second Series. St. Paul: West Publishing, 1928. 388–394. Vol. 9.

McCrystal, James L. "Videotaped Trials: A Primer." Juridicature 61.6 (1978).

McGoorty v. Benhart. North Eastern Reports 2nd series. St. Paul: West Publishing, 1940. 289–296. Vol. 27.

Metz, Christian. *The Imaginary Signifier: Psychoanalysis and the Cinema.* Trans. Celia
    Barton, Annwyl Williams, Ben Brewster, and Alfred Guzzeti. Bloomington: Indiana
    University Press, 1975.
——. *Film Language.* Trans. Michael Taylor. Oxford: Oxford University Press, 1974.
Miller, Ellen J. *Video: A Guide for Lawyers.* Santa Monica, Calif.: Law-Arts Publisher,
    1983.
Miller, Gerald R., and Norman E. Fontes. *Videotape on Trial: A View from the Jury Box.*
    London: Sage Publications, 1979.
"Movies As Evidence." *The New York Times.* February 22, 1920: 8.
Münsterberg, Hugo. *Hugo Munsterberg on Film: The Photoplay: A Psychological Study
    and Other Writings.* New York, Routledge. 2001.
Nichols, Bill. *Blurred Boundeies: Questions of Meaning in Contemporary Culture.*
    Bloomington: Indiana, 1994.
Odin, Roger. "La Semio-Pragmatic du Cinema Sans Crise." *Hores Cadre* 7 (1989).
Partridge. *Origins: A Short Etymological Dictionary of Modern English.* New York:
    Macmillan Publishing Co. Inc., 1966.
Peirce, Charles S. *Philosophical Writings of Peirce.* New York: Dover Publications, 1955.
Powell v. Superior Court. California Appellate Reporter Third Series. St. Paul: West Law,
    1991. Vol. 232.
Rodwick, D. N. *The Virtual After Life Of Film:* Cambridge, Mass.: Harvard University
    Press, 2007.
Rogers, L. S. *Annotation: Use of Motion Pictures as Evidence. American Law Reports
    Annotated.* Vol. 62. Rochester N.Y.: The Lawyers Co-Operative Publishing Com-
    pany, 1958.
Ronell, Avital. "Trauma TV: Twelve Steps Beyond the Pleasure Principle." *Finitude's
    Score: Essays for the End of the Millennium.* Lincoln: University of Nebraska Press,
    1994. 305–328.
Rosen, Philip. "History of Image: Image of History: Subject and Ontology in Bazin." In
    Rites of Realism: Essays on Corporeal Cinema. Ivone Margulies, ed. Durham, Duke
    University Pess, 2003.
Saussure, Ferdinand de. *Course in General Linguistics.* New York: McGraw-Hill Book
    Company, 1959.
Silverman, Kaja. *The Acoustic Mirror.* Bloomington: University of Indiana Press, 1988.
Sobchack, Vivian. *The Address of the Eye.* Princeton, New Jersey: Princeton University
    Press, 1992.
"Society For Cinema Studies Resolution." *Jump Cut.* 37 (1992): 2.
*State for use of Anna Chima v. United Railways & Electric Co. Reports of Cases Argued
    and Adjudged in the Court of Appeals of Maryland.* Baltimore: King Brothers, 1932.
    404–418. Vol. 162.
Strong, John W, ed. *McCormick on Evidence.* St. Paul: West Publishing Co., 1992.
Thomas v. C.G. Tate Construction Co. Inc. Federal Supplement. St. Paul: West Publishing
    Co., 1979. 566–571. Vol. 465.
Wigmore, John Henry. *A Treatise on the Anglo-American System of Evidence in Trials
    at Common Law Including the Statutes and Judicial Decisions of All Juridical
    Jurisdictions of The United States and Canada.* Second ed. Vol. II. Boston: Little,
    Brown, and Company, 1923. IV vols.

Williams, Linda. "Mirrors Without Memories: Truth, History, and The New Documentary." *Film Quarterly* 46.3 (1993): 9–21.

United States of America v. Guerrero. Federal Reporter 2nd Series. St. Paul: West Publishing, 1981. 862–870. Vol. 667.

United States of America v. Weisz and Cuizio. Federal Reporter 2nd Series. St. Paul: West Publishing, 1983. 412–441. Vol. 178.

Usai, Paolo Cherchi. *The Death of Cinema: History, Cultural Memory, and the Digital Dark Age.* London: The British Film Institute, 2001.

Wilson, George M. *Narration in Light: Studies in Cinematic Point of View.* Baltimore: The Johns Hopkins University Press, 1986.

Index

Abscam: 78, 79, 87, 88, 91, 105, 107
Admissibility of motion picture evidence: 17, 27, 29, 30, 31, 32, 33, 34, 35, 80, 86, 90, 100, 123 (fn)
Advanced Litigation Skills Using Video, 93, 95, 97, 100, 101, 102
A. L. Harmon v. San Joaquin Light & Power Corporation, 55, 60, 61
American Law Reports, 1958 note on motion picture evidence, 45, 50, 52, 128 (fn)

Bazin, André, 121 (fn)
Birth, documentary film, 4
Bordwell, David and Kristin Thompson, 121 (fn)
Boyarski v. Zimmerman, 32, 33, 34, 35, 36
Brewer v. Jeep Corporation, 76, 86
Burr, Raymond, 77

California v. Powell et al., 9, 108
Cartwright, Lisa, 121 (fn)
Chima v. Railroad, 23, 30, 31

Coady, C. A. J., 109, 110, 111, 113
Commonwealth v. Roller, 28, 29, 34
Confessions on film or video, 3, 28, 29, 45, 77, 87
Cowley v. New York, 93
Cumulative evidence, 21, 22, 52, 82, 85, 90, 129 (fn)

DeBattiste v. Laudadio, 5, 56, 57, 58, 129 (fn)
DeCamp v. United States, 20, 21, 26
Depositions, 6, 66, 67, 68, 69, 70, 71, 73, 75, 77, 78, 99, 103, 106
Discretion, of the courts, 30, 31, 32, 45, 80, 90, 93
Derrida, Jacques, 116, 123 (fn)
Différance, 117
Doxa. 23, 28, 34, 35, 36, 37, 56, 70

Epistemological approach to film and video, 14, 41, 42
Excluding motion picture evidence, 4, 14, 15, 16, 18, 19, 20, 21, 22, 24, 25, 32, 33, 34, 36, 42, 51, 55, 56, 66, 69, 71, 79, 81, 82, 87, 88, 90, 92, 93, 98, 107, 108, 123 (fn)